W9-ADG-216

AMERICAN CITIES CHRONOLOGY SERIES

PITTSBURGH
A CHRONOLOGICAL & DOCUMENTARY HISTORY

1682-1976

Compiled and Edited by
ROBERT I. VEXLER

Series Editor
HOWARD B. FURER

1977
OCEANA PUBLICATIONS, INC.
Dobbs Ferry, New York

Library of Congress Cataloging in Publication Data

Main entry under title:

Pittsburgh: a chronological & documentary history,
    1682-1976.

    (American cities chronology series)
    Bibliography: p.
    Includes index.
    SUMMARY: A chronology of important events in
Pittsburgh's history accompanied by pertinent
documents.
    1. Pittsburgh — History — Chronology.
2. Pittsburgh — History — Sources. [1. Pittsburgh —
History] I. Vexler, Robert I.
F159.P657P57   974.8'86   77-8948
ISBN 0-379-00606-5

Manufactured in the United States of America

TABLE OF CONTENTS

EDITOR'S FOREWORD

Every effort has been made to cite the most accurate dates in the chronology; various newspapers, documents and letters and chronicles have been consulted to determine the exact data. Later scholarship has been used to verify this information or to change dates when proven plausible.

Because the very nature of preparing a chronology of this type precludes the author from using the standard form of historical footnoting, I should like to acknowledge in this editor's foreword the major sources used to compile the bulk of the chronological and factual materials comprising the chronological section of this work: Leland D. Baldwin, Pittsburgh. The Story of a City; Charles W. Dahlinger, Pittsburgh. A Sketch of Its Early Social Life; George Thornton Fleming, History of Pittsburgh and Environs: From Prehistoric Days to the Beginning of the American Revolution, 2 vols.; Laura C. Frey, The Land in the Fork. Pittsburgh, 1753-1914; Frank C. Harper, Pittsburgh of Today. Its Resources and People, 4 vols.; Erasmus Wilson, ed., Standard History of Pittsburg (sic).

This research tool is compiled primarily for the student. The importance of political, social, economic and cultural events have been evaluated in relation to their significance for the development of Pittsburgh as one of the major cities that have contributed a great deal to the development of the United States. Its citizens were quick to recognize the fine situation they had at the juncture of the Monongahela and Allegheny Rivers, and their connection with the Ohio River system, which would help them to play a major role in the industrial and commercial development of the country. In addition, the discoveries of coal in the immediate vicinity, and iron ore in the environs helped to establish the industrial strength and importance of Pittsburgh. Pittsburgh and the surrounding area have continued to be major suppliers of important industrial equipment and iron and steel for the nation.

Documents have been selected which best illustrate the major aspects in the development of Pittsburgh from the small town in the late eighteenth and early nineteenth centuries to the booming city of the 1970's.

Robert I. Vexler
Briarcliff College

COLONIAL PITTSBURGH

1682   The French laid claim to all the tributaries of the Mississippi and the territory through which they flowed, as a result of La Salle's discovery of the Mississippi.

1712   John Frazier built a trading post near the Monongahela River in the area now occupied by the Edgar Thompson Steel Plant about this time.

1716   The Governor of Virginia became concerned with the French intention to create a military barrier west of the English colonies.

1719   Governor Keith of Pennsylvania urged that a fort be constructed on Lake Erie.

1731   Lieutenant-Governor Patrick mentioned the French threat, and recommended to the Pennsylvania Legislature that a fort be built on Lake Erie.

1744   Representatives of Pennsylvania, Virginia and Maryland met with the Six Nations, and arranged the Treaty of Lancaster. The English based their western territorial rights against the Indians on this treaty.

1748   Thomas Lee, President of the Virginia Assembly, organized the Ohio Land Company to settle the lands about the head waters of the Ohio.

     Conrad Weiser presided over the Council and Treaty with the Indians at Logstown, further confirming the Treaty of Lancaster.

1749   The Governor-General of Canada sent Captain Coleron down the Allegheny and Ohio Rivers to claim possession of the territory for France. Engraved leaden plates were buried at various points. French possession was recorded on August 3.

     Englishmen were trading with the Indians in the region of Pittsburgh.

1750   Christopher Gist blazed a trail over the mountains, and then down the Allegheny River to the Ohio River.

1751   Christopher Gist was present when a treaty
            was made with the Indians at Logstown.

1752   Pennsylvania and Virginia began their long
            boundary dispute.

1753   Christopher Gist guided George Washington,
            who was delivering a message from Governor
            Dinwiddie (dated October 30) of Virginia to
            the Commandant at Fort LeBoeuf. They
            arrived at Pittsburgh on November 24.

            November. James Forbes referred to the
            area as Pittsburgh.

1754   February 17. Captain Trent and forty men
            arrived at Pittsburgh. They had been sent
            by Governor Dinwiddie to the Forks of the
            Ohio. They began to build a stockade which
            may be considered the first settlement at
            Pittsburgh.

            April 17. Captain Contrecoeur and several
            hundred Frenchmen and Indians came down the
            Allegheny. They forced Captain Trent and
            his men to surrender, and to return to Gover-
            nor Dinwiddie, indicating that they were en-
            croaching upon French territory.

1755   Fort Duquesne was built at the "Point" and
            named in honor of the Governor-General of
            Canada.

            The first religious service was conducted by
            the Catholic Chaplain in the chapel of Fort
            Duquesne.

            May 28. George Washington was victorious at
            the Battle of Little Meadows. The French
            commander Jumonville died.

            June 20. Toussaint Boyer died. He was the
            first person to be buried in the Fort ceme-
            tery.

            July 3. The English troops were defeated at
            the Battle of Great Meadows (later site of
            Fort Necessity). George Washington was among
            the troops. Villiers, brother of Jumonville,
            was victorious.

            July 8. General Braddock and his division
            arrived at the junction of the Youghiogheny

and Monongahela Rivers. He was joined by Washington.

July 9. General Braddock was defeated at Fort Duquesne. He died of his wounds three days later.

1756   September. Colonel Armstrong led a successful expedition against the Delaware Indian Village of Kiltaning.

1758   September 14. Major Grant and a detachment of General Forbes' army attacked the French near Fort Duquesne, and suffered a disastrous defeat.

November 24. The French left Fort Duquesne after destroying their stores, and setting fire to the Fort because they could not resist General Forbes.

November 25. General Forbes' army camped on the site of the smouldering ruins of Fort Duquesne. George Washington was one of the officers.

December 3. General Forbes left Pittsburgh with his army. They arrived in Philadelphia on January 17, 1759.

1759   January. The first Fort Pitt was built. Colonel Hugh Mercer was in command.

July. The English, including George Croghan, deputy of Sir William Johnson, met with chiefs and warriors of many Indian tribes to arrange a treaty.

August. General John Stanwix, General Forbes' successor as Commander of His Majesty's troops in the Southern Department came to Pittsburgh.

September 3. General Stanwix supervised the beginning of the construction of Fort Pitt. It was completed in the Summer of 1761.

October 25. General Stanwix, officers of his garrison, George Croghan, Sir William Johnson's representative, and others met with the following Indians: Guyasuta, the King of the Delawares; Shingas, the Pipe; Gustalbo and Kilbuck. They were not able to establish a measure of confidence and understanding.

1760 The first boats were built at Pittsburgh.

July. The first recorded population of Pittsburgh was 464.

July 6. Colonel Burd arrived to relieve Major Tulivers, who had been left in charge of the Fort by General Stanwix.

1761 The people collected more than L60 to pay a schoolmaster to teach more than twenty students.

November. What was probably the first school in Pittsburgh was organized and held in Colonel Burd's house.

1763 May 28. The Indians killed William Clapham and all residents of his house.

June 1. Captain Ecuyer, commandant of the Fort, ordered demolition of the town of Pittsburgh, and took the inhabitants into the Fort.

June 9. George Croghan's house was burned.

June 22. An Indian war party appeared at the farthest extremity of the cleared lands wast of the Fort.

June 23. The Indians approached the Fort. Turtle's Heart, a Delaware chieftain, addressed the garrison.

June 26. Another parley occurred between the Indians and the garrison.

August 5. The Indians attacked some troops. Sixty men were killed and injured, Colonel Henry Bouquet defeated the Indians at the battle of Bushy Run.

August 11. Colonel Bouquet ended the Indian siege of the Fort, and thereby this aspect of Pontiac's Conspiracy.

1764 Colonel John Campbell made the first survey of Pittsburgh.

Summer. A Block House was built in the Fort

with a tablet engraved "Col. Bouquet, A.D. 1764."

1765   Billiard tables were first introduced into Pittsburgh.

May 15. George Croghan left Fort Pitt to go west as instructed by General Gage. He was bringing gifts to the Indians in order to gain their friendship.

1766   Coal was used in the Fort.

September 5. Reverend Charles Beatty, who was appointed by the Synod of New York and Philadelphia to visit the frontier, arrived in the evening. He preached to the garrison on September 7. His companion, Mr. Duffield, preached to the people.

1768   April and May. A conference was held at Pittsburgh with the Six Nations, the Delawares, Munsies and Mohickens, who complained of encroachment upon their lands. Nothing was accomplished.

October 24. Sir William Johnson presided at a conference at Fort Stanwix, New York. New Jersey, Pennsylvania and Virginia also sent commissioners to meet with the chieftains of the Six Nations, the Shawnees and Delawares. Thomas and Richard Penn paid $10,000 for Indian lands lying west of the Susquehanna River, including the disputed territory of Pittsburgh and surroundings. A land office was opened in Pittsburgh the following Spring.

1769   January 5. A warrant was issued to survey the manor of Pittsburg.

February 23. An advertisement was published that the land office would open April 3.

March 27.The survey of Pittsburgh was completed. It was found to contain 5,766 acres.

April 3. The land office opened in Pittsburgh to sell the land bought from the Indians.

1770   October 17-20. George Washington stopped
              at Pittsburgh on a journey to the territory
              he owned in the west.

1771   The Penns appointed Arthur St. Clair,
              Aeneas Mackay, Devereux Smith and Andrew
              McFarbane magistrates in Westmoreland
              County, which included almost all of Western
              Pennsylvania.

              June 1. Brigadier General Hand took over
              the Fort from Captain John Neville.

1772   October. General Gage ordered Major
              Edmundson to abandon Fort Pitt as a result
              of the Penn purchase in 1768.

1773   April 6. The first court in Western Penn-
              sylvania was held at Hannastown.

              April 9. Dr. John Connolly took possession
              of Fort Pitt under orders from Governor
              Dunmore of Virginia, and renamed it Fort
              Dunmore.

1774   September 17. Lord Dunmore was in Pittsburgh
              preparing for his expedition against the
              Indians. He issued a proclamation that the
              area was to be considered part of Virginia.

1775   A ducking stool was built at the Point.

              February 21. Virginia held the the first
              court at Pittsburgh.

              May 16. Citizens attended a meeting which
              approved the actions of the New Englanders
              in resisting the tyranny of the British
              Parliament. They also approved the develop-
              ment of friendship with the Indians.

              August 7. The Virginia Provincial Council
              ordered Captain John Neville to take possess-
              ion of Fort Pitt. He and his troops reached
              the Fort on September 11.

              August 25. John Campbell was called before
              a committee and admitted to having tea. He
              surrendered it, and it was burned at the
              Liberty Pole.

1776   July. A conference was held with the Indians
              to gain their friendship. Guyasuta guaran-

teed that his people would not allow the
Americans or the British to march an army
through his territory.

October. The counties of Yohogania, Monon-
gahelia and Ohio were created. Pittsburgh
was in Yohogania County.

1777   February 23. Thirteen boat carpenters arrived from Philadelphia to build boats to
transport troops to fight the Indians.

1778   Spring. Fort Pitt was reinforced. General
McIntosh took command, and General Hand
returned to the East.

June. The Continental Congress ordered that
a conference with the Delawares be held at
Fort Pitt on July 23. It was postponed until September.

Summer. Fort McIntosh was built at the
mouth of Beaver Creek.

September 12. A conference with the Dela-
wares was held within Fort Pitt. By the
terms of the treaty arranged, the United
States entered into an alliance with the
Delawares, recognizing their independence.
It was signed September 17.

October 8. Fort McIntosh was made the headquarters for the army of the Western Department.

1779   March. Colonel Daniel Brodhead succeeded
General McIntosh as commander of the Western
Department.

August. Colonel Daniel Brodhead led a successful expedition against the Munsies and
Senecas in the northern part of Pennsylvania.

August 31. At a meeting in Baltimore, the
bitter boundary dispute between Pennsylvania
and Virginia was amicably settled. The a-
greement was ratified by the Virginia Legislature on June 23, 1780, and the Pennsylvania
General Assembly on September 23, 1780.

1780   Iron ore was discovered in the Western
Alleghenies.

1781   October. General William Irvine took command of Fort Pitt and brought an end to the
chaos which was evident there.

November 6. Cornwallis' surrender was reported at Fort Pitt.

1782   Summer. General Irvine had Fort Pitt re-
paired.

1783   September. William Butler was granted the
right to run a ferry between Pittsburgh
and Allegheny.

October. General Irvine retired after his
garrison was furloughed as a result of the
conclusion of peace with Britain. Major
Joseph Marbury remained in charge of Fort
Pitt with a small detachment.

1784   David Elliot was given the right to run a
ferry from Saw Mill Run to the opposite
bank of the Ohio.

Colonel George Woods and Mr. Vickroy sur-
veyed Pittsburgh. Woods laid out the plan
for the "Triangle for the Penns."

1785   September. The General Assembly passed an
act providing $8,000 for a state road between
Miller's Spring and Pittsburgh.

December 24. The Freemasons were chartered
in Pittsburgh as Lodge No. 45 of the Ancient
York Masons.

1786   Hugh Ross established the first ropewalk.

July 29. John Scull and Joseph Hall began
publication of the Pittsburgh _Gazette_.

November 15. Mrs. Pride opened a boarding
school and day school for young ladies in
John Gibson's former house.

1787   John Penn and John Penn, Jr. donated two and
one-half lots for the building of Trinity
Church. The deed was filed at Greenburg in
1788. They also gave lots for the Presbyterian Church, chartered that year, and a
German Evangelical Church.

John Scull began publishing the _Pittsburgh_

Almanac.

The first postal service was established.

February 28.   The Pennsylvania General
Assembly incorporated the Pittsburgh Academy.
Judge Hugh Henry Brackenridge was the chief
promoter.

March 1.   Hugh Ross, Stephen Bayard and
Reverend Samuel Barr were appointed a committee to propose a plan for construction of
a market house.   They presented their report
on March 12.   The Market House was soon built
at Second Avenue and Market Street.

September 24.   The Penns granted two and one-
half lots to the Hon. John Gibson, Esq.,
John Ormsby, Devereux Smith and Dr. Nathaniel
Bedford as trustees of the Episcopalian
Protestant Church.

September 29.   The Pennsylvania legislature
incorporated a Presbyterian Congregation
in Pittsburgh.

November 11.   The town of Allegheny, which
was later merged with Pittsburgh as the
Northside, was laid out.

1788   The first circulating library was established.

January 5.   Thomas Towsey opened a school
for boys.

March 24.   A local branch of the Mechanical
Society, a social and educational organization for workers, was established.

April 3.   The May Flower, the first boat with
New England emigrants bound for the mouth of
the Muskingham, arrived in Pittsburgh.   This
was the beginning of an emigration which
added many people to the territory.

July 7.   William Tilton was appointed the
first postmaster.

September 24.   The Assembly created Allegheny County.

1790   John Hayden found iron ore in Fayette County.

November 1. The Alliance Iron Works first
fired their furnace.

1791   Congress passed legislation placing an excise tax on whiskey from nine to twenty-five
cents a gallon according to its strength.
This was to cause a great deal of unrest in
the west.

The Pennsylvania General Assembly passed an
act appropriating $25,000 for construction
of a road from Bedford to Pittsburgh.

April 13. An Act was passed by the State
legislature providing for the purchase of
land in Pittsburgh to build a courthouse
and prison.

September 5. Robert Johnson, excise collector for Allegheny and Washington Counties,
was waylaid and tarred and feathered.

1792   George Anshutz built the first iron furnace
near Pittsburgh -- three miles from its
boundaries.

Henry Brackenridge published the first volume
of Modern Chivalry. The fourth and last
volume was issued in 1813.

At a mass meeting, the federal whiskey tax
was denounced.

1793   The volunteer Pittsburgh Fire Company was
formed.

The courthouse and jail was completed.

October 14. Jacob Meyers began packet service between Pittsburgh and Concinnati every
other week.

PITTSBURGH AS A BOROUGH

1794   April 22. Pittsburgh was incorporated as
a borough.

May 19. The first town officers were elected, including George Robinson and Josiah
Tannehill as chief burgesses.

May 21. The first regular meeting of the

newly elected town council was held.

July 19. A town meeting was held at which
it was decided to establish a second Market House on the bank of the Monogahela River at the foot of Market Street.

August 1. Seven thousand men gathered in a
rebellion against the federal whiskey tax.

August 7. President George Washington issued
a proclamation ordering the insurgents to
lay down their arms before September 1, or
they would suffer grave consequences. He
also began to raise an army.

August 14-15. At a meeting at Parkinson's
Ferry, Henry Brackenridge was able to modify
some of the demands for immediate action concerning the whiskey tax.

August 20. General Anthony Wayne completely
routed the Indians at Fort Deposit, thereby
relieving Pittsburgh from future devasta-
tions and raids.

October 1. President Washington and an army
of 12,000 started out for Pittsburgh to put
down the Whiskey Uprising.

November 9. Many men active in the Whiskey
Rebellion, including sixteen at Pittsburgh
were arrested. Henry Brackenridge was not
on the list although many of his political
enemies hoped that he would be removed.

November 17. General orders were issued for
the return of the federal troops except one
detachment under General Morgan, which was to
remain in Pittsburgh for the winter.

November 19. The army began to return to the
East taking with it many prisoners.

November 29. General Henry Lee issued a
general amnesty for all but a few citizens
involved in the Whiskey Rebellion.

1795   Jacob Bowan began producing nails in his
              factory at Brownsville.

1797   Major Isaac Craig and General James O'Hara
              began manufacturing glass.

April 16. A meeting of citizens resolved to purchase fifty fire buckets as part of their campaign against fires.

1798   A special act of the Pennsylvania General Assembly permitted the establishment of a lottery to raise money to build docks along the Allegheny River.

The citizens raised $400 for the yellow fever victims in Philadelphia.

May 19. The President Adams, commissioned by Congress in 1797, was launched.

June 28. An ordinance was passed ordering the Burgesses to divide the town into two or more companies for working and keeping the fire engine in order.

July 14. A meeting was held to improve the organization of the militia because of probable trouble with France and England. Some of those present expressed their anger over the conduct of the French toward the United States.

October 15. Mr. McDonald opened an evening school for young men.

1799   Benjamin F. Brewster opened a night school in the Academy.

Spring. The Senator Ross, ordered by Congress in 1797, was launched.

1800   The population was 1,565.

August 4. The Tree of Liberty, a weekly paper, was first published.

1801   Zadoc Cranmer began publication of The Ohio and Mississippi Navigator.

Peter De Clary gave voice and instrumental music lessons in the court house.

August 1. An ordinance was passed to lay out pathways paved with brick, stone or gravel, and bounded by curbstones of lumber.

October 14. John Taylor, Rector of the old Episcopal Church, opened a night school.

1802   August 9. The Town Council ordered that
                four wells be sunk in order to increase the
                water supply.

1803   James O'Hara built the Pittsburgh Point
                Brewery.

                January. E. Carr opened a school for child-
                ren of both sexes.

                William Porter established the first iron
                foundry in Pittsburgh.

                January 5. Robert Steele opened a school,
                after having left the faculty of the Pitts-
                burgh Academy.

                March 26. The Freeholders and other inha-
                bitants met at the courthouse to establish
                a branch of the Bank of Pennsylvania. It
                opened on January 9, 1804.

1804   The Second Presbyterian Church was organized.

                Peter Eltonhead opened the first cotton
                factory.

                March 5. The General Assembly passed an act
                reincorporating the Borough of Pittsburgh.

                March 17. Elections were held for town
                officers.

                May. William James opened a school.

                July 4. Ephraim Pentland issued the Common-
                wealth, the first Democratic paper in
                western Pennsylvania.

                The first stage line offering regular ser-
                vice to and from Philadelphia was estab-
                lished, with one stage leaving each end
                of the line once a week.

1805   The Episcopalians organized a congregation.

                April. Aaron Burr visited Pittsburgh.

1806   May. Newspapers published advertisements
                for bids to construct the turnpike from
                Pittsburgh to Harrisburg.

                August. Aaron Burr visited Pittsburgh again,

and discussed his ideas for a western empire
with several young men.

December 14. Fourteen young men, including
Morgan Neville and William Robinson, left
Pittsburgh to join Aaron Burr's troops at the
mouth of the Cumberland in their attempt to
take over the West.

1807   March. The General Assembly incorporated the
          Harrisburg, Lewistown, Huntington and Pitts-
          burgh Turnpike.

1808   February 24. Samuel Kingston announced the
          opening of a school on April 6.

          July 1. The cornerstone of Trinity Church
          was laid.

          August 10. Rev. William M'Kindry, Jr.,
          Bishop of the Methodist Episcopal Church,
          preached at the house of Thomas Cooper.

1809   The first steam flouring mill was built.

1810   A great flood caused considerable damage.

          Birmingham, later the South Side, was set-
          tled.

          The Second Bank of Pittsburgh was organized
          as the Pittsburgh Manufacturing Company.
          Its name was changed on June 16, 1812. It
          continued in existence until 1931.

1811   March. The New Orleans was launched. It was
          the first steam boat built at Pittsburgh.
          It made its first trip up the Monongahela
          River in September.

          Summer. Thomas Hunt opened a school for
          women.

          July. James C. Gilleland began publishing
          the Mercury, which soon absorbed the Common-
          wealth.

          September 30. J. Graham announced that he
          would open a select school. He was delayed
          in this endeavor, but announced that he
          would open a school on April 1, 1812.

1812   Mrs. Gazzam opened a seminary for young

ladies.

Mr. Aquila M. Bolton opened an academy for young ladies in his house.

Z. Phelps opened an English school.

January 18. Rev. Taylor began to deliver a course of lectures on astronomy in the Long Room.

February. The Pioneer, a monthly journal, was first published.

August. John C. Brevost, a Parisian, opened a school to teach French.

August 2. An express post (five days) was established by the government from Washington to Detroit through Pittsburgh.

August 12. The citizens of Pittsburgh met in response to the declaration of war against Great Britain, June 18, 1812. They appointed a public safety committee.

1813   Susan Dalrymple opened a sewing-school across the Monongahela River.

The Pittsburgh Humane Society was established.

July 8. William R. Thompson opened a circulating library.

November 27. The first recorded meeting of the Pittsburgh Permanent Library Company was held at William McCullogh's house. Books were first offered for rent on April 15, 1814.

1814   The Allegheny Arsenal was established at 39th Street. It manufactured munitions in large quantities during the Civil War.

The Pittsburgh Franklin Society was organized to encourage patriotism.

May 10. The Bank of Pittsburgh opened as the Pittsburgh Manufacturing Company.

July. The Presbyterian Banner was established at Chilicothe, Ohio. It moved to Pittsburgh in 1819.

August 2. The Farmers' and Mechanics' Bank
was organized with $450,000 in capital.
John Scull was the first president.

October. Mrs. Brevost and her daughter opened
a young ladies' boarding school.

1815   The Pittsburgh Bible Society was organized
to spread the word of God among the poor.

THE CITY OF PITTSBURGH

1816   Bayardstown and Lawrenceville were laid out.

Charters were granted for the construction of
the first bridges over the Monongahela and
Allegheny Rivers.

The first street lights, whale oil lamps,
were put up, but were soon taken down because
they were constantly being broken.

March 18. Pittsburgh was incorporated as a
city. It was divided into two wards. The
following officers in addition to the Mayor
and Aldermen were provided for: a high constable, four constables, a captain of the
watch and twelve watchmen.

Summer. The Adelphi Free School was established by a group of benevolent women.

July 9. Ebenezer Denny was elected the
first mayor of Pittsburgh. He resigned
July 23, 1817.

1817   A branch of the Bank of the United States
was established.

April 1. The night watch was abolished as
an economy measure.

July 31. John Darragh was elected Mayor
following the resignation of Ebenezer Denny.
Mayor Darragh served until 1825, when he resigned on June 20.

September 5. President James Monroe visited
Pittsburgh.

Fall. Mr. Boardman opened a school for boys.

1818   The _Statesman_ was first published with
            Ephraim Pentland, editor.

            The turnpike was completed from Pittsburgh
            to the Ohio River.

            W.B. Foster and William Hamilton petitioned
            the Council for the privilege of supplying
            the City with water for the inhabitants
            and utilities.

            William and Robert Moody established
            Moody's Academy.

            January. The Pittsburgh Musical Society was
            organized at William Evans' house.

            Fall. The proprietors of "Harmonie" estab-
            lished a seminary for young ladies.

            December. The Monongahela Bridge was opened
            at the foot of Smithfield Street.

1819   The Mechanics and manufacturers of the city
            and surrounding territory, organized the
            Pittsburgh Manufacturing Association to
            promote domestic industry.

            The Pittsburgh Navigation and Insurance Com-
            pany was incorporated.

            The Union Rolling Mill was built. It was
            the first to puddle iron and roll iron bars.

            February 19. Governor William Fenley signed
            the charter of Western University of Penn-
            sylvania. When the inhabitants of
            Allegheny opposed the use of their pasture
            land, the buildings of the Pittsburgh
            Academy were repaired and given to the new
            university in the Spring of 1820. Eventually
            its name was changed to the University of
            Pittsburgh.

1820   The population was 7,248.

            The _Statesman_ was first published. It be-
            came the _Pennsylvania Advocate_ and _Statesman_
            in 1837.

            The first Allegheny River Bridge, the Sixth
            Street or St. Clair Bridge was opened. It
            was replaced in 1860 by a suspension bridge.

Spring. Rev. Joseph Stockton opened a school.

1821   Cook and McClelland discovered iron six miles from Washington, Pennsylvania.

March 31. The state Legislature authorized the Allegheny County Commissioners to employ teachers to educate the poor free of charge.

June. The Pittsburgh Medical Society was organized.

1822   The banking house of Nathaniel Holmes was established. It later became N. Holmes and Sons, and was merged into the Union National Bank in 1905.

February. The Weekly Recorder, first issued on July 5, 1814, was moved to Pittsburgh, and called the Pittsburgh Recorder. It absorbed the Spectator on January 10, 1829, took over the Christian Herald in 1833, the the Presbyterian Advocate in 1838, and the Presbyterian Banner and Advocate on November 17, 1855. Its name was changed to the Pittsburgh Banner on March 10, 1866.

1824   John McFarland founded the Allegheny Democrat.

An ordinance providing for construction of a waterworks system was passed. It was completed in 1828 but did not operate efficiently.

1825   May 30-June 1. General Lafayette visited Pittsburgh.

June 28. John M. Snowden was elected Mayor by the Councils after John Darragh resigned. Mayor Snowden served until January 8, 1828.

December. The Allegheny Seminary was founded, and opened in Allegheny. It later became the Pittsburgh Theological Seminary.

1826   The General Assembly passed a bill authorizing the building of the Pennsylvania Canal.

The State Prison was completed at a cost of $183,092.

July 4. Stephen Foster, the great American songwriter, was born in Pittsburgh. He went to Cincinnati in 1848.

November 12. The first number of The Western Journal was issued.

1827   The Western Theological Seminary, Presbyterian, was opened.

The Allegheny Democrat, a weekly paper, was first issued. It became the Allegheny Democrat and Workingman's Advocate in 1837, and united with the Mercury in 1841.

William Griffiths had an ordinance passed giving him exclusive right to light the City with gas.

The Pittsburgh and Coal Hill Turnpike was begun.

N. Ruggles Smith first published The Hesperus, a monthly literary journal.

The Baltimore and Ohio Railroad received a charter from the Pennsylvania Legislature giving it fifteen years to extend the line to Pittsburgh.

1828   The Crystal, a literary magazine designed for women, was first issued.

January 28. Magnus M. Murray was elected Mayor and served until 1830.

April. I. I. Gurnsey opened the St. Clair Female Academy.

April 14. Allegheny and Birmingham were incorporated into boroughs.

July. John W. Young began publication of the Jackson Free Press.

December. The first water works went into operation.

1829   January. The Liberal Catholic, or Weekly Remembrancer, was first issued.

February. The Pittsburgh Reading-room was
established.

April 23. The Northern Liberties became a
borough.

June. Mechanics' Lodge No. 9, Independent
Order of Odd Fellows, was organized.

June 24. The cornerstone of the new Catholic
Church was laid.

August 5. The Anti-Masonic Party of Allegheny County was organized.

August 20. Robert Fee began publication of
The Independent Republican.

November 10. The first canal boat, General
Lacock, arrived at Pittsburgh on the Pennsylvania Canal.

December 4. The City was divided into four
wards: North or Allegheny, South or Monongahela, East or Grant, and West or Point.

1830   The various temperance societies formed a
union, and began an active campaign.

Oil lamps were installed on the streets
again.

Samuel P. Reynolds opened an academy in
Robinson's Row in Allegheny.

G. and J. Smith opened an evening school
and a day seminary.

January 12. Matthew B. Lowrie was elected
Mayor, and served until 1831.

January 30. Citizens met at the court house
and petitioned the State Legislature to
draft a uniform law for schools.

March 6. William B. McConway began publication of the American Manufacturer.

March 26. A large temperance meeting was
held in the City.

1831   The first steam ferry appeared.

The Associate Congregation of Pittsburgh, Presbyterian, was chartered.

January 11. Magnus M. Murray was elected Mayor, serving until 1832.

January 12. The _Pittsburgh_ _Times_ first appeared.

June 23. Books were opened for six days for subscriptions to the stock of the Washington and Pittsburgh Railroad at Nicholas Griffith's Hotel.

August 27. The National Republicans met in Pittsburgh, and nominated Henry Clay for President and William Wirt for Vice President.

November 1. The Edgeworth Ladies' Boarding School announced that it would open the following Monday. It continued in operation until about 1868.

December. The citizens of Pittsburgh passed resolutions at a meeting, inviting the Baltimore & Ohio Railroad to consider Pittsburgh as its western terminus.

1832   The Pittsburgh and Allegheny Orphan Asylum was organized in Allegheny.

J. J. Gillespie opened an art gallery and store.

The _Advocate_ was first published.

The Pittsburgh Savings Fund Company was opened.

January 10. Samuel Pettigrew was elected Mayor. He served until 1836.

February. The blacks of Pittsburgh and vicinity organized the Pittsburgh African Education Society.

October. A cholera epidemic broke out.

October 2. The first notice of the Western Female Collegiate Institution appeared.

1833   Rev. Charles Elliott began editing the _Pitts-_

burgh _Conference_ _Journal_. Its name was
changed to the _Christian_ _Advocate_ in 1841.

H. Williams opened his writing academy.

Daniel Stone opened a literary and scientific institute for boys。

Daniel Webster visited the city.

The _Friend_, a weekly publication of the Young
Men's Society, was begun under the editor-
ship of J. W. Nevin.

Government deposits were removed from the
branch of the United States Bank.

The fire companies of Pittsburgh and Allegheny formed a general association for mutual benefit and assistance.

The Merchants' and Manufacturers' Bank was
chartered with Michael Tiernan as president.
It was reorganized under the National Bank
Law as the Merchants' and Manufacturers'
National Bank. It was absorbed by the Bank
of Pittsburgh, N. A. in 1904.

February. William H. Van Doren opened a
school.

March. The Third Presbyterian Church was
organized.

May. Cholera reappeared.

June. _Der_ _Pittsburger_ _Beobachter_ began publication.

July 1. The first number of _The_ _Saturday_
Evening _Visitor_ was issued by Ephraim Lloyd.
It was later absorbed by the _Daily_ _American_.

July 30. Neville B. Craig made the _Gazette_
a daily as the _Daily_ _Pittsburgh_ _Gazette_.

Summer. The first humane society in Pittsburgh was organized.

September 2. The "Old Drury" Theatre was
opened with a performance of _Hamlet_.

October 4. The Pittsburgh Anti-Slavery Society was formed.

1834   The Legislature had amended the charter
in 1833. The Mayor was to be elected by
the people rather than by the Councils.

The canal aqueduct was completed at Eleventh
Street. It was replaced by a suspension
aqueduct in 1845, which was said to have been
the first of its kind in the world.

The Pittsburgh Savings Fund Company was organized with Thomas Fulton as president. It
became the Farmers' Deposit Bank in 1841, and
was reorganized as a National Bank in 1865.

January 11. A historical society was formed
at a meeting in Mr. George Beale's Long Room.
Thomas Bakewell was elected president. It
lasted a few years and then was revived in
1843, and dissolved once again. Its successor was the Historical Society of Western
Pennsylvania founded in 1877 and chartered
in 1888.

April. The charter for the first Board of
Trade was issued.

April 1. Governor Wolf approved Act No. 102
establishing a general system of common
school education in Pennsylvania.

April 15. The Firemen's Insurance Company
was incorporated.

April 16. The canal to Pittsburgh was completed.

May 4. St. Paul's Catholic Church was dedicated.

June 28. The citizens met in each of the
four wards to elect school directors.

August. I. Fletcher opened a gymnasium or
school for athletic exercises.

November. The first school delegate meeting
was held, where it was decided to levy a
tax of $6,500.

1835   The first public school opened in Pittsburgh
with five pupils.

January. Samuel Pettigrew was elected Mayor.

1836   The Monongahela Navigation Company was
        formed, and was granted state aid to build
        dams and locks along the river.

        The Exchange Bank was organized with
        $1,000,000 in capital, and William Robinson,
        Jr. was chosen as its first president. It
        became the Exchange National Bank in 1836.

        Professor E. S. Blake opened an English and
        classical school.

        An act was passed to build a bridge over the
        Allegheny River at Hand Street.

        January. Thomas R. McClintock was elected
        Mayor, and served until 1839.

        January 16. Rev. Samuel William issued the
        first number of The Christian Witness, an
        antislavery paper.

        March. An act was passed to incorporate a
        company to build a bridge over the Allegheny
        River at Mechanic Street.

        March 26. The night watch was revived by the
        City Council. A captain, two lieutenants and
        sixteen watchmen were hired.

        The City Council passed an ordinance to re-
        duce the grade or "Hump" in the downtown
        district. Some work was done, although not
        a great deal.

        April. Rev. Nathaniel Todd established the
        Pittsburgh and Allegheny English and Classi-
        cal Seminary.

1837   A fifth ward was added to the City, The
        Northern Liberties or Bayardstown.

        Victoria Scriba brought the Freiheits Freund,
        a German paper, to Pittsburgh from Chamber-
        lain, Pennsylvania. It had been founded in
        1834.

        Dr. Gustavus Reichhelm introduced Homeopathy
        in Pittsburgh.

        The Hand Street Bridge over the Allegheny was

built.

William Larimer and William Robinson, leading a group of Pittsburgh citizens, received a charter to build a railroad from Pittsburgh to Connellsville.

Specie payment was suspended during the Panic.

January. The Gazette refused to publish an advertisement for a runaway slave at the request of a Tennessee slave-holder.

March 31. The Monongahela Navigation Company received a charter.

April 5. The City was first lighted by gas.

December. The St. Clair Street Bridge was lighted with gas for the first time.

1838   Sibbert's Western Review, a monthly journal concerned with financial and commercial news, began publication.

The Pittsburgh Institute of Arts and Sciences was incorporated.

The Mechanic's Bridge was opened at Sixteenth Street. It burned in 1851 and was rebuilt.

October. A convention of anti-slavery societies was held in Pittsburgh.

1839   The Commercial Bulletin and American Manufacturer, a weekly paper, was first published.

The Volksblatt, a German paper, was first published.

Other publications first issued were the Whig paper, the Daily American, an afternoon paper and successor to the Saturday Evening Visitor; Harris' Intelligencer; Victoria Scriba's The Pittsburgh Entertainer, a German weekly.

The following magazines were first published: The Literary Examiner and Western Monthly Review, and the Sabbath School Assistant.

William Little was elected Mayor.

1840   The Old Drury Theater failed financially.
            It was reopened in 1842. It finally closed
            January 1, 1870.

            The Odeon Society, an important musical or-
            ganization, was founded.

            James and John B. Kennedy began publication
            of The Express, a Whig paper.

            The Pittsburgh and Beaver Canal opened.

            Allegheny became a city with a population of
            10,089.

            Peter Duff established Duff's Mercantile
            College.

            January. William W. Irwin was elected Mayor.

            May 29. The new bridge from Hand Street
            across the Allegheny to Cedar Street was
            completed.

            June. The Daily Whig first appeared.

1841   Millvale became a borough.

            The private banking houses of Cook & Cassat,
            E. Sibbett & Co., Sibbett & Jones, and Allen
            Kroner were established.

            Alexander McIlwane and John C. Ivory began
            publishing The Literary Messenger. Other
            publications first issued were The Missionary
            Advocate and The Reformed Presbyterian and
            Covenanter, both monthlies; The Pittsburgh
            Herald and Weekly Advertiser, and the Pitts-
            burgh Intelligencer, both weeklies.

            Daniel McCurdy first issued The Daily Sun.

            B. Guenther began editing the German paper,
            The Free Press.

            The Mercury and the Allegheny Democrat were
            consolidated.

            The Pittsburgh Atheneum, a reading room and
            library, opened.

            January. James Thompson was elected Mayor.

March 31. The Pennsylvania Insurance Company
was organized.

April. The first Monongahela House opened.
It burned down in the fire of 1845.

May. R. G. Bereford began publishing The
Pittsburgh Chronicle. It merged with the
Evening Telegraph in 1884 as the Chronicle-
Telegraph.

1842   The Mercury and the Allegheny Democrat absorbed the American Manufacturer. It was
the origin of the Daily Post.

The Preacher, a semi-monthly Reformed Presbyterian magazine, was first published. It
became a weekly in 1848, and was continued
as the United Presbyterian.

The second court house was completed at a
cost of $200,000.

January. Alexander Hay was elected Mayor.
He served until 1945.

September 10. William H. Smith and Thomas
Phillips issued the first number of The
Daily Post.

March 28. Charles Dickens and his wife began their visit to Pittsburgh.

1843   The third jail was completed.

April 19. The first number of The Spirit
of the Age was published.

August 7. The Diocese of Pittsburgh was
formed. Rev. Michael O'Conner was consecrated its first bishop at Rome on August 15,
1843. He resigned in May, 1860.

1844   The second waterworks system was put into
operation.

Dorothea Dix visited Pittsburgh, and began
work for legislative reform in the treatment
of the insane and physically ill. She began
to collect funds for the Western Pennsylvania
Hospital, which was chartered in 1848.

St. Paul's Catholic School opened.

March 16. The <u>Pittsburgh</u> <u>Catholic</u> began
publication.

Summer. The Allegheny Cemetery Association
was formed.

1845   The night watchmen stopped calling the hours.

The <u>Daily</u> <u>Morning</u> <u>Ariel</u>, a Democratic journal, was first published.

The banking house of Hill & Carny was established.

Daniel Bushnell first towed coal by steam-
boat on the <u>Walter</u> <u>Forward</u>.

January. William J. Howard was elected
Mayor.

April 10. Fifty-six acres of Pittsburgh were
destroyed in a great fire.

PITTSBURGH AFTER THE GREAT FIRE

1846   Rodef Shalom Temple, oldest Jewish congregation in the city, was organized. Its members
worshipped in a room over the engine room of
the Vigilant Fire Engine Company.

The State Legislature decided to authorize
both the extension of the Baltimore and Ohio
Railroad and the Pennsylvania Railroad, if
the latter had a subscription of three million dollars in stock by July 30, 1847.

The Monongahela River was spanned by a wire
suspension bridge designed by John Roebling
would would later design the Brooklyn Bridge
in New York City.

N. B. Craig began editing the <u>Olden</u> <u>Time</u>.

January. William Kerr was elected Mayor.

February 8. Col. J. H. Foster established
<u>The</u> <u>Dispatch</u>.

December 29. The first telegraph communication was opened with the East by the Atlantic
and Ohio Telegraphic Company.

1847   Dr. H. D. Sellers presided over a meeting
        which formed an association to establish The
        Western Pennsylvania Hospital. It received
        its charter on March 18, 1848 and opened in
        January, 1853.

        The Evening Day Book was first published.

        January. Gabriel Adams was elected Mayor,
        and served until 1849.

        January 1. Mercy Hospital, founded by Bish-
        op O'Conner, was opened in Penn Street. It
        was incorporated as a charitable institution
        in 1882.

        Spring. The new Monongahela House, a hotel,
        was opened on the site of the former hotel
        of the same name.

        July 13. The first record of the Mercantile
        Library Association appeared on this date.

1848   Andrew Carnegie came to Allegheny with his
        family.

        Alex B. Russell first published the monthly
        Odd Fellow magazine, The Token.

        South Pittsburgh became a borough.

        The Scientific Association of Western Penn-
        sylvania was organized in the hall of Western
        Pennsylvania University.

        January. Gabriel Adams was reelected Mayor.

        February. Mr. Youngson first issued the
        Sunday Mercury.

        March. The Western Pennsylvania Hospital
        was incorporated. It opened in 1853.

        Spring. Henry Clay visited Pittsburgh.

1849   The Pittsburgh Infirmary, the first Protes-
        tant Hospital, opened. It was later called
        Passavant Hospital.

        Duquesne Borough was formed. It merged with
        Allegheny in 1868.

        Charles Avery founded a training school for

"colored" children.

An outbreak of smallpox occurred.

The Pittsburgh and Wheeling Railroad was incorporated.

January. John Herron was elected Mayor.

July. Allegheny firemen refused to put a fire out in a carpenter shop because the City Council would not increase their appropriation. They stopped companies from Monongahela and Pittsburgh from helping. The fire burned thirty-five buildings including a Presbyterian Church.

August. President Zachary Taylor, and Pennsylvania Governor Johnson visited Pittsburgh.

1850   The population was 46,601.

Stephen Foster married Jane Denny McDowell, daughter of Dr. Andrew N. McDowell of Pittsburgh.

January. Joseph Barker was elected Mayor. He attacked the saloons and the inefficiency of the police, and constantly criticized the City Councils. He even had Bishop O'Conner arrested because of the poor condition of the sewer from Mercy Hospital to Stevenson Street.

April 26. The Associated Firemen's Insurance Company of Pittsburgh was incorporated.

1851   The Pittsburgh and Ohio Railroad was completed to Beaver.

Masonic Hall was completed.

A crime wave of theft and arson occurred.

January. John B. Guthrie was elected Mayor, and served until 1853.

The Mechanic Street Bridge over the Allegheny River was burned as a result of arson.

April 25. Jenny Lind first sang in Pittsburgh at the Masonic Hall.

July 1. The first locomotive for the Pittsburgh and Ohio Railroad arrived by canal.
It was called "The Salem."

July 30. The Ohio and Pennsylvania Railroad
first ran locomotives out of Pittsburgh. It
was opened as far as New Brighton. Several
months later, a connection was made with the
Cleveland and Cincinnati Railroad, which then
permitted the beginning of rail transportation between Pittsburgh and Cleveland.

1852   The Fifth Ward Savings Bank was founded with
James Loughlin as President. It purchased
the Pittsburgh Trust and Savings Company. On
July 18, 1863, the Pittsburgh Trust Company
was organized as the First National Bank of
Pittsburgh. It made the first application
under the National Bank Law, and became the
first to be so recognized.

The Citizens' Bank was formed, becoming a National Bank in 1865. In 1902 the Union Trust
Company purchased and liquidated the bank.

The Baltimore and Ohio Railroad opened.

The Federal Government opened a marine hospital for rivermen at Woods Run.

A Board of Health was established.

January. The Pittsburgh Trust and Savings
Company was organized with a capital of
$150,000. Its name was changed to the Pitts-
burgh Trust Company in 1853.

January 22. Louis Kossuth visited the City.

May. R. D. Hartshorn and W. S. Havens first
issued the Union Artisan, which was concerned
with agriculture, horticulture and mechanics.

August. The National Free Soil convention
was held in Pittsburgh. Many prominent figures, including Salmon P. Chase, Frederick
Douglass and Charles Francis Adams were
present.

November 29. The Pennsylvania Railroad o-
pened between Pittsburgh and Philadelphia,
although the Columbia and Portage Railroads
had to be used for part of the distance. By

1854, with the completion of the mountain
division, the Pennsylvania's own trains covered the three hundred miles within thirteen
to seventeen hours.

1853   The Catholic Diocese of Pittsburgh was divided. Erie became the new See.

Dr. David Alter, physician and chemist,
ground a prism from a fragment of flint glass
taken from the ruins of Bakewell's glass-
house. He eventually developed spectrum
analysis.

Work began on the Allegheny Railroad.

Allegheny's gas lighting system was put
into use.

The borough of West Pittsburgh was created.

The Post Office and Government Building was
erected on the corner of Fifth Avenue and
Smithfield Street.

January. Robert M. Riddle was elected Mayor.

1854   Another epidemic of cholera broke out killing
249 people.

A House of Refuge for juvenile offenders was
opened.

"Uncle Tom's Cabin" first played in Pittsburgh.

The use of iron for the exterior structure
of buildings was begun.

The Republicaner, a German paper, was first
issued.

The Board of Trade was reorganized.

January. Ferdinand E. Volz was elected Mayor. He served until 1856.

February 10. The Pittsburgh Female College
was incorporated. It was run by the Methodist Episcopal Church, and continued in
existence for fifty years.

Spring. The Young Men's Christian Association was organized.

May. The State Free Soil Convention met in Wilkin's Hall.

1855 The Mechanics' Bank was established with a capital of $500,000. It became a national bank in 1865, and was absorbed by the First National Bank in 1902.

October. Bishop O'Conner established a Catholic Theological Seminary.

1856 Construction of a bridge across the Allegheny was begun to connect the Fort Wayne and Pennsylvania Railroads. It was not completed until 1858, because of a dispute in regard to laying tracks across Pennsylvania Avenue.

The Allegheny Railroad was opened.

January. William Bingham was elected Mayor.

February 22-28. The first National Republican Convention was held at Lafayette Hall. The time and place of the national convention to nominate a President and Vice President were fixed at Philadelphia on June 17, 1856.

1857 The Allegheny Bank was established with H. Hepburn as president, and a capital of $500,000. It became the Allegheny National Bank in 1864.

The Public Works (Canals) were purchased by the Pennsylvania Railroad Company for $7,500,000.

January. Henry A. Weaver was elected Mayor, and served until 1860.

1858 The Mechanics' Bridge burned and was rebuilt.

Monongahela Borough was created.

January. The law requiring that the mayor, treasurer and controller be elected biennially, by general vote, went into operation.

Mayor Weaver was reelected.

May 26. At the City Hall, the First United

Presbyterian Church (Scotch-Irish) was
formed through a union of the Associate and
Associate Reformed Churches.

1859   The Pittsburgh and Birmingham Passenger Railroad Company was chartered.

Temperanceville became a borough.

A separate institution for the insane, a
branch of Western Pennsylvania Hospital, was
opened at Dixmont at the suggestion of Miss
Dorothea Dix.

The Union Banking Company was formed with
John R. McCune as president and a capital of
$250,000. It was reorganized as the Union
National Bank in 1864.

The Pittsburgh, Allegheny and Manchester
Railway was built from Pittsburgh across the
Allegheny River, through Allegheny, and on
to the borough of Manchester.

January 10. The Western Pennsylvania Historical Society held its first stated meeting
at the Merchants' Exchange.

March. The Citizens Passenger Railway to
Lawrenceville was built as the first street
railway.

August 28. The first oil well was brought
in causing great excitement.

October. Graff, Bennett and Company built
the first blast furnace in Allegheny County.
It was fired this month.

1860   Professor Lewis Bradley collected money to
start work on the Allegheny Observatory.

January. George Wilson was elected Mayor,
and served until 1862.

May 10. The Roebling Suspension Bridge, replacing the Allegheny Bridge, was opened for
travel.

October 2. The Prince of Wales, later Edward
VII of England, visited the City.

December 9. Rt. Rev. M. Domenec was conse-

crated Bishop of Pittsburgh. He was trans-
ferred to Allegheny, January 11, 1876.

December 14. Secretary of War Floyd ordered
the removal of the cannon from the Arsenal.

December 27. The citizens of Pittsburgh resolved to prevent the removal of the cannon
from the Arsenal.

1861   The Pittsburgh and Allegheny Home for the
Friendless was organized.

The Pittsburgh and Birmingham Bridge was
opened.

February 14-15. President-elect Abraham
Lincoln visited the City.

April 12. News of the fall of Fort Sumter
arrived in the City.

April 15. At a mass meeting, resolutions in
support of the Union and against the rebels
were passed. A Committee of Public Safety
was to be formed.

April 17. The Turner Rifles, the first Union
Troops from Pittsburgh, left for the front.
The Committee of Public Safety was named.

May 9. The Commercial Journal was merged
with the Gazette.

1862   The Pittsburgh Bank for Savings, James Park
president, was organized with a capital of
$75,000.

The banking house of Robinson Brothers was
established.

Bishop Brown Institute was established by
Rev. Dr. Van Dusen, Rector of St. Peter's
Protestant Episcopal Church.

January. Benjamin C. Sawyer was elected
Mayor, and served until 1864.

September 17. An explosion in the Allegheny
Arsenal killed eighty people.

1863   The Scientific School of Western University
was founded. A bachelor's degree could be

obtained.

The Third National Bank was formed with a
capital of $300,000 and Adam Reinemann as
president.

June 14. During the Gettysburg campaign the
people feared that the Confederates would
capture the City. Therefore, the manufacturers and businessmen met at the Monongahela House, where they agreed to stop business, and have the men prepare for defense.

1864   The People's National Bank was organized with
a capital of $1,000,000.

The Fourth National Bank of Commerce was
formed with a capital of $500,000. It was
absorbed by the Mellon National Bank in 1903.

The Tradesmen's National Bank, Alexander
Bradley, president, was established with a
capital of $400,000.

The Commercial was first published.

January. James Lowry was elected Mayor and
served until 1866.

January 13. Stephen C. Foster, the famous
songwriter, died in New York City in the
charity ward of Bellevue Hospital.

February. The first twenty-inch gun ever
made, was cast in Pittsburgh at the Fort
Pitt Foundry.

February 13. The Second National Bank, formerly the Iron City Trust Company, obtained
a charter. G. E. Warner was the first president. The bank had a capital of $300,000.

June 1. A Sanitary Fair was opened.
$363,570.09 was raised for the establishment
of a Soldiers' Home.

September. The Bankers' and Brokers' Board
was organized consisting of twenty-five
banking and brokerage houses.

October 14. Andrew Carnegie formed the first
of his iron companies, the Cyclops Iron
Company.

December.   John W. Pitcock began publication
of the Sunday Leader.

1865   The Mechanics Bridge was destroyed by a
            flood, and was rebuilt.

            Andrew Carnegie formed the Keystone Bridge
            Company, for which the Cyclops Iron Company
            supplied the iron.   This, and subsequent
            companies were part of the iron and steel
            empire he created.

            The Panhandle Railroad opened.

            The City Deposit Bank and Trust Company was
            formed with Dr. John Q. Marchand as presi-
            dent.   It later became the City Deposit Bank.

            February.   The Pittsburgh School of Design
            for Women was opened.

            March 6.   The People's National Bank was or-
            ganized with a capital of $1,000,000.   Thomas
            Mellon was president.   In June, 1903, it be-
            came a part of the Safe Deposit and Trust
            Company.

            April 15.   The City received news of the
            assassination of President Lincoln.

            April 20.   The Allegheny County Medical So-
            ciety was organized.

            May.   The bankers met to establish a clearing
            house.   It was formally created in June by
            eighteen banks.   It opened for business on
            February 5, 1866.

            August.   Street letter boxes were set up
            in various parts of the city.

            October 4.   General Ulysses S. Grant visited
            Pittsburgh.

            October 30.   The St. Francis Hospital was
            organized.

            PITTSBURGH AFTER THE CIVIL WAR

1866   The managers of the Allegheny Observatory
            turned it over to the Western University.

January. William C. McCarthy was elected Mayor and served until 1868.

A Stock Exchange was established.

April 4. The Pennsylvania Legislature granted a charter for the Homeopathic Hospital. Its board of trustees was elected on April 9, 1866, and it opened August 1.

September 13. President Andrew Johnson, Admiral Farragut, and General Grant visited the city.

1867   The Coal Men's Trust Company was formed with W. G. Johnston president. Its name was changed to the Duquesne Bank in 1872, and then it became the Duquesne National Bank in June, 1875.

The East End was annexed.

The Pittsburgh Petroleum Association was formed.

January 24. The Safe Deposit and Trust Company was incorporated under a perpetual charter. It became the Pittsburgh Safe Deposit and Trust Company in 1884.

March 12. The boroughs of Manchester and Duquesne were annexed to Pittsburgh.

1868   The Federal Street and Pleasant Valley Street Railway line was incorporated.

The Central Passenger Railway was organized.

The Masonic Deposit Savings Bank was formed with $200,000 in capital. It was reorganized as the Lincoln National Bank in April, 1893.

Oakland and Lawrenceville were annexed to Pittsburgh.

The Ewalt Street Bridge was built.

January. James Blackmore was elected Mayor.

January 8. The Fort Pitt Banking Company was organized with a capital of $200,000. Its first president was Samuel McClarkum. It was reorganized as the Fort Pitt National

Bank in 1879.

June 20. St. Francis Hospital was incorporated.

1869   The Workingman's Savings Bank of Allegheny
        was organized with a capital of $50,000 in
        stock on the individual liability plan. It
        became a state bank in April, 1897.

        The private banking house of T. Mellon and
        Sons was organized by Judge Thomas A. Mellon.
        His son Andrew joined the firm in 1874, and
        Richard a few years later. In 1889 Andrew
        Mellon and some associates established the
        Union Transfer and Trust Company with Andrew
        as president. It became the Mellon National
        Bank in 1902, and absorbed the Pittsburgh
        National Bank of Commerce in 1903. Then, in
        September, 1946, the Union Trust Company was
        merged with the Mellon National Bank and be-
        came the Mellon National Bank and Trust
        Company.

        January. Jared M. Brush was elected Mayor
        and served until 1872 since the mayor's term
        was extended to three years.

        April 13. The patent for the Westinghouse
        Air Brake was issued to George Westinghouse.
        He founded the Westinghouse Air Brake Company
        in the same year. In 1890, the Company's
        Wilmerding plant was built fourteen miles
        from Pittsburgh.

        September 14. President Grant visited
        Pittsburgh.

1870   The population was 86,076.

        The State Legislature passed an act estab-
        lishing a paid fire department.

        Andrew Carnegie founded Carnegie, Kloman and
        Company.

        The Enterprise Savings Bank was organized
        with a capital of $100,000. It was reorgan-
        ized under a state charter in 1872, and be-
        came a national bank in 1895.

        The Pittsburgh and Ormsby Passenger Railway
        Company was granted a charter.

The Grand Opera House was built, and continued in operation until May, 1903.

March. The Freehold Bank and Building Association was opened. It became the Freehold Bank in 1879.

April 8. The Germania Savings Bank was chartered with a capital of $150,000.

October 11. The Evening Leader first appeared.

1871
A pesthouse was erected on 34th Street. It was the beginning of the South Side Hospital.

The Arsenal Bank of Pittsburgh was organized. It opened with a special charter granted March 20, 1873.

The Diamond Savings Bank was established. It was reorganized as the Diamond National Bank in 1875.

The Pittsburgh and Connellsville Railroad connected with the Baltimore and Ohio Railroad at Cumberland.

Andrew Carnegie established Carnegie & Co.

March. The German Savings and Deposit Bank was organized with a capital of $80,000.

November 15. The first number of The Western Recorder, first issued as the Methodist Recorder in July, 1839, appeared.

1872
Work began on the new water works.

The Legislature passed an act merging all the South Side boroughs with Pittsburgh.

The new City Hall was completed.

Andrew Carnegie organized the Keystone Bridge Company, Incorporated.

January. James Blackmore was elected Mayor and served until 1875.

March. The Traders' and Mechanics' Bank was organized as the Odd Fellows" Savings Bank. The name was changed in July, 1878.

The district south of the Monongahela, consisting of 27.7 square miles, was annexed to Pittsburgh.

The Iron and Glass Dollar Savings Bank of Birmingham received its charter.

March 14. The Farmers; and Mechanics' Bank of East Birmingham was incorporated. It was rechartered October 4, 1884 as the Manufacturers' Bank of Pittsburgh.

1873   The Fifth National Bank came into existence.

The Duquesne Club was organized.

The Art Society of Pittsburgh was incorporated.

The Pittsburgh Free Dispensary was organized and incorporated.

Andrew Carnegie formed Carnegie, McCandless & Co.

April 10. The General Assembly of Pennsylvania passed an act annexing Birmingham to Pittsburgh. It was to take effect January 1, 1874.

April 16. The first issue of the Evening Telegraph appeared.

1874   The Western Pennsylvania Humane Society was organized.

Andrew Carnegie established The Edgar Thomson Steel Company. Steel manufactured by the Bessemer process was begun.

April 29. The Pittsburgh Dental College was incorporated. It merged with Wesleyan University on April 16, 1896.

1875   Natural Gas was first used for manufacturing in Pittsburgh.

January. William C. McCarthy was elected Mayor, serving until 1878.

April 30. The German National Bank of Allegheny was organized.

December 15.   The Pittsburgh Association for
the Improvement of the Poor was organized.

1876   The Catholic Diocese was divided again, and
Allegheny became the new Episcopal City.

The _Pittsburgh Bulletin_ was established as
the oldest illustrated journal in western
Pennsylvania.

The Western Pennsylvania Institution for the
Instruction of the Deaf and Dumb received
$16,000 from the State Legislature, and
opened a home for those so afflicted.

The Union or Point Bridge was opened.

March 19.   Rt. Rev. J. Tuigg was consecrated
Bishop.

July 8.   The Chamber of Commerce was chartered and supplanted the Board of Trade.
The Hon. Thomas M. Howe was the first president.

1877   The Academy of Music was opened for thea-
trical productions.

Andrew Carnegie formed the Lucy Furnace
Company.

The first public exhibition of electric
lights was shown on Duquesne Heights.

July 19.   The railroad strike, which had be-
gun at Baltimore on the Baltimore and Ohio
Railroad on July 16, spread to Pittsburgh.
The militia was initially called out, and the
Pennsylvania National Guard on July 20.   The
mob had gained control of the City.

July 23.   Citizens formed a Committee of Public Safety to protect themselves, as a result
of the riots caused by the railroad strike.
Order was finally restored.

August.   The Catholic Dioceses of Pittsburgh
and Allegheny were reunited.

1878   The telephone was introduced into the city.

Duquesne University was founded by the Holy
Ghost Fathers.

January. Robert Liddell was elected Mayor, serving until 1881.

1879   Andrew Carnegie formed The Pittsburgh Bessemer Steel Company, Limited.

The Pittsburgh and Lake Erie Railroad was opened.

The Old Residents' Association of Pittsburgh and Western Pennsylvania was organized. It became the Historical Society of Western Pennsylvania in 1882.

1880   Mrs. Felix Brunit, Miss Jane Holmes and Miss Jane B. Holmes organized the Home for Colored Children between the ages of two and twelve.

The Allegheny General Hospital was established.

Robert P. Nevin began publication of the Times, a morning penny newspaper.

March 6. The Allegheny Light Company was founded with the Pennsylvania Railroad as its first customer. Arc lights, mounted on poles in the train yards, were used to prevent looting.

1881   Andrew Carnegie offered Pittsburgh $250,000 for a free public library on condition that the city provide $15,000 annually for its maintenance. It was not immediately accepted.

January. Robert W. Lyon was elected Mayor, serving until 1884.

1882   Andrew Carnegie founded Wilson, Walker and Company.

May 7. The second court house burned down.

October 18. The Allegheny General Hospital was granted a charter by the Court of Common Pleas of Allegheny County.

1883   The Pittsburgh Press was founded by Col. Thomas M. Boyne.

John H. Dether founded the Illustrated Star.

The Protestant Orphan Asylum was organized.

Andrew Carnegie organized Hartman Steel Company, Limited.

September 24. The first Sunday edition of the _Dispatch_ was issued.

1884   The Duquesne Theater was built. It was remodeled in 1907.

The Seventh Street Bridge was completed.

January. Andrew Fulton was elected Mayor.

August. The Americus Club, Republican, was organized. It was incorporated in 1886.

1885   The Protestant Home for Incurables, incorporated in 1883, opened on Butler Street.

The Home for Aged and Infirm Colored Women was incorporated.

March 15. The Pittsburgh Newsboys' Home was formed.

August 2. Rt. Rev. Richard Phelan was consecrated Bishop.

1886   The Fidelity Title and Trust Company was organized with William O. H. Scully as its first president.

George Westinghouse first entered the electrical manufacturing industry.

Carnegie, Phipps and Company, as well as the Duquesne Steel Company, were established.

The Medical Department of the Western University was established.

May. The new jail was finished, but was not occupied until September.

May 13. George W. Shuman presented a resolution in the City Council offering Mr. Carnegie the Third Ward Diamond Square as a site for the free library. The City would agree to the terms of the 1881 offer to provide $15,000 annually, if Carnegie gave $500,000. He said he would spend $250,000, and later made it $300,000.

1887   The Western Pennsylvania Institution for the
        Blind was established.

        The State Legislature passed an act accepting
        Andrew Carnegie's gift for a new library. In
        the winter of 1890, Carnegie said he would of-
        fer $1,000,000 if Pittsburgh would appropri-
        ate $40,000 per year for the maintenance of
        the library. The City passed an ordinance
        accepting the proposal on May 31, 1890. The
        building was dedicated on November 5, 1895.

        January. William McCallin was elected Mayor,
        serving until 1890.

        March 18. The Pittsburgh Hospital for Child-
        ren, built through the generosity of Miss
        Jane Holmes, was incorporated.

1888   Charles M. Hall, who had taken out a patent
        for refinement of aluminum in 1886, came to
        Pittsburgh seeking money for his process.
        His pioneer plant on Smallman Street was the
        beginning of the Aluminum Company of America.

        Andrew Carnegie helped to organize the Alle-
        gheny Bessemer Steel Company.

        April. The third court house was completed.

        May 1. The Monongahela National Bank was
        chartered with a capital of $250,000, and
        Thomas Jamison as president.

1889   Mrs. Mary Schenley gave the city its first
        park, which eventually grew into 400 acres
        next to the civic center at Oakland.

        October 28. The Union Transfer and Transit
        Company was incorporated with Andrew W. Mel-
        lon as its first president. The charter was
        amended in 1902 under the name of Union Trust
        Company of Pittsburgh.

        December 7. Rt. Rev. J. Tuigg was consecra-
        ted Bishop.

1890   The Young Women's Christian Association was
        organized in the Fourth Avenue Baptist
        Church.

        The building for the Western Pennsylvania
        Institution for the Blind was opened.

The Bethesda Home for fallen women was
opened.

The Pennsylvania National Bank was chartered
with a capital of $200,000, and J. S. Seamen
as president.

January. Henry I. Gourley was elected Mayor.

February 20. The Carnegie Library in Allegheny was dedicated.

April 29. The Liberty National Bank was
organized with a capital of $200,000. John
H. McKelvey was the first president.

May 26. The Dollar Savings Bank and Trust
Company of Allegheny was chartered with a
capital of $125,000. John W. Chalfont was
its first president.

1891   Andrew Carnegie established Carnegie, Phipps
& Company, Limited, as part of his iron and
steel empire.

June 4. The Pittsburgh Hospital for Children
was first opened as the Shadyside Cottage
Club. It was incorporated March 18, 1887.

June 10. The Pittsburgh Chapter of the
Daughters of the American Revolution was or-
ganized largely through the efforts of Mrs.
Julia K. Hogg.

1892   The Sunday Post was first issued.

Carnegie Steel Company, Limited was formed.

June 1. A merger of the Western University
and the Western Pennsylvania Medical College
was arranged.

July 1. The Homestead Strike broke out a-
gainst the Carnegie Steel Company. Andrew
Carnegie was spending the summer in Europe,
at his palace in Scotland as usual. Henry
Frick, who was left in charge, claimed that
he was not able to receive any communication.

July 6. Henry Frick sent the Pinkerton De-
tective Agency's men up the river to the Carnegie plant, five miles from Pittsburgh, to
protect the works.

July 11. Carnegie regained control of his
plant, when Governor Pattison ordered 8,000
Pennsylvania National Guardsmen, led by Major
General George Snowden, to go to Homestead
to restore order.

1893   The Curtis Home for Destitute Women and Girls
            was organized as a result of the effort to
            aid those who were suffering from the Panic
            of 1892.

            January. Bernard McKenna was elected Mayor,
            serving until 1896.

            March 10. The organization of the Pittsburgh
            Trust Company was arranged with a capital of
            $600,000.

            May 23. The Columbia National Bank was char-
            tered with a capital of $300,000. Edward
            H. Jennings was its first president.

            September. The National Bank of Pennsylvania
            was organized with James Hemphill as presi-
            dent. It had a capital of $300,000.

1894   The Academy of Our Lady of Mercy was founded.

            The Kingsley House was founded to carry out
            settlement work. Dr. George Hodges, rector
            of Calvary Church, was instrumental in its
            organization.

            July 24. The Consolidated Traction Company
            was chartered as a part of the merger of the
            street railways of Pittsburgh. One hundred
            eighty-seven miles of track were taken over.

            October. The Twentieth Century Club was or-
            ganized. It was a philanthropic, civic, and
            literary club for women.

1895   The East End Theater was built.

            The School of Mines and Mining Engineering
            became a part of the Western University.

            June 22. The Eye and Ear Hospital of Pitts-
            burg was organized.

            October 3. The Pittsburgh Law School joined
            Western University.

November 1. The Carnegie Library building, the beginning of Pittsburgh's Public Library System, was dedicated.

1896   The Pittsburgh Hospital was organized.

January. Henry P. Ford was elected Mayor, serving until 1899.

February 27. The first season of the Pittsburgh Symphony Orchestra was begun in Carnegie Music Hall.

March. The Daily News first appeared.

April 16. The Pittsburgh College of Pharmacy became affiliated with Western University.

April 20. The first charter was granted to the Dental College, and by an agreement with the trustees of Western University, the College became its Dental Department.

July 27. The United Traction Company was chartered and took over one hundred fifty-seven miles of street railways in the city.

1897   February 26. Walter S. Lobingier issued the first number of the Pittsburgh Index.

1898   May 11. The Lawrenceville Branch Library opened.

1899   January. William J. Diehl was elected Mayor. He served until 1901.

January 13. An ordinance for the widening of Diamond Alley was passed. The work was completed in 1904.

February 1. The West Branch Library opened.

June 1. The Wylie Avenue Branch Library opened.

1900   The population was 321,616.

The Southern Traction Company was chartered to absorb the lines of the West End Traction Company consisting of 48.8 miles.

The Mayee Pathological Institute was founded.

March. The Carnegie Company was formed after Carnegie Steel Company, Limited was purchased and consolidated with the H. C. Frick Coke Company. Operations of the company began April 1, 1900 and ended March 31, 1901, when the company's resources were sold to the United States Steel Corporation. Carnegie received $250,000,000 in U. S. Steel Corporation 5% gold bonds.

May 31. The Mount Washington Branch Library opened.

August 16. The Hazelwood Branch Library opened.

November 15. Andrew Carnegie gave the city $1,000,000 to establish a technical institute if the city would provide the land. Over the years, he gave a total of $36,000,000 to the Institute.

PITTSBURGH IN THE TWENTIETH CENTURY

1901   Major Adam M. Brown was City Recorder for a few weeks.

J. O. Brown was elected Recorder under the provisions of the new City Charter. He served until 1903.

George Westinghouse began production of a single-phase alternating current variable-speed motor, which was suitable for interurban railway service.

The Homewood Bank was organized with a capital of $50,000. It was absorbed by the Guarantee Title & Trust Company in 1913.

April 1. The East End Board of Trade was chartered. It was the initial step in the formation of the Pittsburgh Board of Trade.

April 15. The South Side Company of Pittsburgh was organized with a capital of $300,000. Benjamin Page was the first president.

May 31. The People's Trust Company of Pittsburgh was organized with a capital of $250,000.

May 15. The Moreland Trust Company was organized and later absorbed by the Guarantee Title and Trust Company.

July. The Oakland Bank was organized with $50,000 in capital.

July 10. The Allegheny Trust Company was organized with a capital of $700,000. It opened in September.

July 17. The Realty Trust Company was incorporated. Its name was changed to the Iron City Trust Company, October 9, 1902.

November 10. The first Sunday Gazette was issued.

1902
January 30. The Colonial Trust Company was organized with a capital of $1,000,000. It became the Colonial National Bank on January 7, 1903. It merged with the American Trust Company, August 10, 1903.

July 14. The Union Savings Bank opened with a capital of $1,000,000. Henry C. McEldowner was president.

October 17. The Potter Title and Trust Company was organized with a capital of $200,000. John F. Potter was its president.

November 10. The Merchants' Savings and Trust Company with a capital of $500,000 opened.

1903
The Nixon Theater was built and opened.

The South Hills Trust Company was organized with a capital of $125,000.

January. W. B. Hays was elected Recorder and served about one week. Under the new charter revision, which provided for a mayor once again, Hays ran for Mayor, and was elected, serving until 1906.

March 9. The Real Estate Savings and Trust Company of Allegheny was chartered with a capital of $200,000.

April 22. The Continental Trust Company, which was chartered in February, opened with a capital of $500,000.

July 27. The Builders' League merged with the Builders' Exchange. The new organization took the name of Builders' Exchange League.

September 17. The Merchants and Manufacturers' Association of Pittsburgh was begun. A permanent organization was created February 17, 1904, and its charter was granted April 25, 1904.

1904   The Wabash Railroad was opened.

September 20. St Joseph's Hospital was opened.

December 20. Rt. Rev. J. F. Regis Canevin was consecrated Bishop.

1905   The first department of the Carnegie Technical School opened.

The Metropolitan Trust Company was incorporated.

October 10. The East Liberty Branch Library opened.

October 16. The School of Applied Science for young men was opened with the aid of a two million dollar donation by Andrew Carnegie.

1906   The College of Physicians and Surgeons was founded for exchange of medical information.

January. George W. Guthrie was elected mayor and served until 1909.

February 7. The City of Allegheny was annexed by the Greater Pittsburgh Act of the Legislature.

March 1. The _Post_ issued its evening edition called the _Sun_.

June 12. Allegheny residents voted no, and Pittsburgh residents, yes, for the merger. A majority of votes were cast in favor of the merger. The courts declared on June 16 that Allegheny was officially a part of Pittsburgh.

The *Times* merged with the *Gazette* as the *Gazette-Times*.

1908   June. The Montefiore Hospital was opened.

The first diplomas were granted to students graduating from Carnegie Institute.

1909   Arsenal Park, the site of the old Allegheny Arsenal, was given to the city by the United States government.

William A. Magee was elected Mayor and served until 1913.

January 30. The South Side Branch Library opened.

1910   Mr. John Kowalski, a boat builder, constructed a Curtiss-type biplane.

March 10. Homewood Branch Library opened.

1911   A young Pittsburgher, Galbraith Perry Rodgers made the first transcontinental flight on record, from New York to California, taking 49 days to accomplish this feat.

1913   April 21. School children struck because of their opposition to the methods of Superintendent of Schools Sylvanus L. Heeter.

April 23. A coal mine explosion killed 120 miners.

June 2. Superintendent of Schools Heeter was found guilty of immorality, and was dismissed June 6.

November 4. Joseph G. Armstrong was elected mayor.

1914   January 12. Mayor Armstrong banned boxing.

February 18. Mayor Armstrong ordered that sexes be separated at motion picture shows.

April 1. Policewomen were appointed to the secret service division of the police force.

April 6. In an Irish riot, "Patsy" Brannigan was badly beaten in a battle with some Ulster men.

December 4. The councilmen cut their own salaries as a result of the business down-turn.

1915   July 12. A bureau of censorship for magazines was established.

November. James Thompson was elected mayor.

December 12. Iron molders went on strike in the munitions plants.

1916   April 21. The United Mine Workers ordered 24,000 miners in the Pittsburgh district out on strike, because promised wage increases had not been granted. The miners were ordered back to work by the Union on April 26.

April 30. The Pittsburgh Street Railways Company employees went out on strike. They finally accepted a compromise, and returned to work May 2.

May 23. Fifty thousand coal miners in the Pittsburgh district went out on strike again because of their disatisfaction with the agreement with the mine owners, especially the open-shop agreement.

August 11. The formation of the Pittsburgh, Cincinnati, Chicago and St. Louis Railroad was brought about by consolidation of various roads.

November 28. The price of all afternoon newspapers was raised.

1917   November 3. Mayor Thompson announced that a meatless day would be instituted to help the war effort.

November 6. Edward V. Babcock was elected mayor. He served until 1921.

December 2. All textbooks containing positive references to the German Emperor or the German military system were ordered removed.

1918   July 14. The Sunday newspaper prices were raised to ten cents.

1919   Casper P. Mayer established Mayer Field, Pittsburgh's first airport in Bridgeville.

It continued to be the only one until 1922.

May 14. A walk-out of three thousand employees followed a disagreement to submit a
wage dispute to the War Labor Board.

June 5. J. Johnson, President of the International Workers of the World, was arraigned
with fourteen other suspects for bombings.
They were sentenced to prison.

August 14. A strike against the Pittsburgh
Railway Company broke out. Riots eventually
occurred over the use of strikebreakers. The
managers stopped this last practice on
August 25.

December 10. The _Pittsburgh_ _Post_ was issued
with no display advertisements, and only
twenty pages, because of the shortage of
newsprint.

1920   The population was 588,343.

February 3. The dancehall proprietors formed
an organization to suppress improper dancing.

November 2. KDKA of the Westinghouse Electric and Manufacturing Company began broadcasting. It was the first broadcasting
station in the world.

November 11. The World War veterans refused
to parade past Mayor Babcock because he had
permitted "tag day" for the relief of German
children.

1921   February 3. The Pittsburgh Employers' Association began an open shop campaign.

April 19. Mrs. Margaret S. Gray took up her
duties as Superintendent of the Bureau of
Recreation.

November. William A. Magee was elected mayor.

1922   Rodgers Field was established at Aspinwall
as the city's municipal airfield as a result
of the efforts of the Aero Club.

January 24. The policemen and firemen were
ordered to withdraw from the Fraternal Order

of Police and the Firemen's Protective Association, as well as the American Federation of Labor.

September 14. A bust of William Pitt, presented to the American people by the British Sulgrave Institution, was unveiled in Pittsburgh.

1923   February 23. The Pittsburgh <u>Dispatch</u> was sold.

1924   June 2. The Business-District Branch Library opened.

1925   Pittsburgh's first commercially owned airport was established by Mr. D. Barr Peat and associates. It was called Beltis Field.

July 22. Race riots occurred in Pittsburgh.

October 14. The Pittsburgh Pirates, National League Champions, won the seventh game of the World Series and the baseball championship. They defeated the Washington Senators.

November. Charles H. Kline was elected Mayor.

1926   The Government awarded Clifford Ball a contract to carry air mail between Pittsburgh and Cleveland.

May 2. Mayor Charles Kline was reported to have threatened to dismiss any city employee who failed to support the Pepper-Fisher ticket.

October 10. The police broke up all Sunday games except tennis and golf.

1927   Frick Park, given to the city by Henry C. Frick, was opened.

February 26. Police Lieutenant Callan and Patrolmen Lavery and Moran were convicted in Federal Court of assaulting V. Brown and other dry agents, who were trying to identify a policeman seen in a raided place.

July 8. The Citizens' League of Pittsburgh and Allegheny County requested that Mayor Charles H. Kline remove Superintendent of

Police Peter P. Walsh because he tolerated
vice.

July 23. Mayor Kline rejected the Citizens'
League demand for the dismissal of Walsh,
and attacked William L. King, the League's
director.

August 1. George S. Oliver, president of
the Newspaper Publishing Company in Pittsburgh, announced the sale of the Gazette-
Times and the Chronicle-Telegraph to William
Randolph Hearst.

Paul Block bought the Pittsburgh Post and the
Sun from the Post and Sun Publishing Company.
He then sold the Sun to Hearst, and bought
the Gazette-Times from Hearst. He announced
that he would publish the merged paper as
the Post-Gazette.

November. An International Coal Conference
was held in Pittsburgh.

October 1. The Pirates won the National
League Pennant.

October 9. The New York Yankees won the
World Series, defeating the Pirates, four
games to none.

November 7. William L. King resigned as
director of the Citizens' League. His wife
had filed suit for divorce on October 26.

1928   January 21. The Sunday concerts of the
Pittsburgh Symphony Society were held lawful.

February 7. Eastern Air Lines applied for
a permit to begin Pittsburgh-New York passenger service.

May 19. The price of the Pittsburgh Sun-
Telegraph was raised to three cents.

June 9. A Federal Grand Jury indicted 167
persons, including city officials, for involvement in a "rum ring."

July 12. The Pittsburgh Symphony Society
won a Superior Court decision over the blue
laws, which had been used as an attempt to

prevent its Sunday concerts.

July 18. The Knoxville-Carrick Branch Library opened.

November 2. The Grand Jury indicted 224 people on charges of graft, including some policemen.

1929   June. A group of women, sentenced for election frauds, described ballot stuffing and illegal voting as practiced in the Homestead election of 1926.

August. Clifford Ball began air passenger operations, carrying passengers along with mail to Cleveland.

August 3. The Public Welfare Department organized the Accident Research Association in cooperation with the National Safety Council, and the University of Pittsburgh.

September 17. Charles H. Kline was reelected Mayor.

October 5. A Grand Jury recommended legislative reforms of the registration procedure, and censured the Tax Assessment Board.

1930   January 30. The Pittsburgh Real Estate Board announced that it would cooperate with federal prohibition officers in preventing the use of rented buildings for the sale and manufacture of intoxicating liquors.

October 23. A boulevard was named KDKA after the radio station.

December. The two-thirds majority clause in the charter defeated the metropolitan plan.

1931   April 2. A broadcasting station and ballistic laboratory were added to the Police Department equipment.

June 25. Mayor Kline and Bertram L. Succop, deposed director of the Department of Supplies, were indicted because of scandals in the latter department.

September 14. Seven thousand names were

stricken from the registration lists.

October 17. It was announced that three
thousand Public Works Department employees
would get two week vacations, without pay,
in order to cut the land tax.

October 31. Eleven thousand five hundred
names were stricken from the registration
lists.

1932   May 14. Mayor Kline, and former Director of
the Department of Supplies, Bertram L. Succop, were convicted of irregularities in
municipal purchases.

September 10. A Grand Jury investigation revealed corruption in the city government.

September 15. Mayor Charles Kline was declared innocent of the charge of malfeasance
in office. Bertram L. Succop's conviction
was upheld.

1933   January 25. Mayor Kline was ordered back to
the lower court for action on the malfeasance
charge.

March 1. Mayor Kline was sentenced to six
months imprisonment for malfeasance in
office.

March 27. Mayor Kline was removed from office by a court order. He announced that he
would resign.

April 8. Acting Mayor John S. Herron announced his administration aims, and indicated he would seek a full term.

November 7. William McNair was elected Mayor.

1934   April 21. The National Economy League formed
the Efficiency and Economy Committee of
Pittsburgh.

July 18. Mayor McNair asked city employees
to withdraw from unions as a protest against
general strikes.

October 13. Postmaster General James Farley
dedicated the Post Office Building.

1935 February 16. The House received a bill to oust Mayor McNair, and the Senate received a bill for the adoption of a City Manager Charter.

1936 June 13. The Court offered a Grand Jury investigation of the Police Department. Mayor McNair was arrested when he ordered the magistrates to stop the hearings. Sheriff Frank I. Gollmer was appointed emergency Guardian of public safety.

  June 15. Mayor McNair revoked the order furloughing Safety Director Thomas A. Dunn.

  October 6. Mayor McNair resigned when the City Council refused to confirm his appointment for a new City Treasurer. Cornelius Scully was appointed Mayor pending his election.

  October 19. Cornelius Scully was elected Mayor by the City Council.

  November 17. William McNair attempted to rescind his resignation. The Court of Common Pleas ruled, on this date, that McNair could not withdraw his resignation, and that Cornelius Scully was legally mayor.

1937 November 2. Cornelius Scully was reelected mayor.

1939 January 31. The city government announced that it would take over operations of the Keystone Hotel in order to gain back taxes.

1940 The population was 671,659.

1941 September 22. Truck and equipment drivers struck the city in spite of the Council's pleas that it was short of funds. The strike was settled September 24.

  November 4. Mayor Scully was reelected.

1942 January 15. Mayor Scully's reelection in 1941 was upheld in the courts.

  April 2. Various civic groups protested Mayor Scully's dismissal of Recreation Director Louis C. Schroeder.

October 11. The police gave handcuffs to
the Federal Government for Axis prisoners.

1943   June 19. A proposed wartime merger of the
Pittsburgh Steelers and Philadelphia Eagles,
National Football League teams, was approved
because of a player shortage.

June 4. Mayor Scully lost his gasoline ra-
tions for his private and official cars, because he violated the rules. He was able
to ride to work in another city-owned auto-
mobile.

1944   January 13. It was announced that the Philadelphia Eagles and the Pittsburgh Steelers
would operate independently.

The City Council passed a resolution to offer
a daily prayer for United States servicemen.

1945   September 24. Councilman Thomas J. Gallagher
proposed that three thousand city-owned lots
be sold to servicemen.

November 6. David L. Lawrence was elected
Mayor. He served from 1946 to 1958.

POST WORLD WAR II: REDEVELOPMENT OF THE CITY

1946   May 1. J. Lester Perry urged that local
industry in Pittsburgh be diversified so that
there could be more growth in the city.

1947   May 20. Women patrolmen began to take on
traffic assignments.

December 18. Leading business executives
presented a redevelopment plan to prevent
future slumps in the city's economic situation.

1948   June 19. The Pennsylvania Supreme Court upheld the city's mercantile and personal property taxes.

October 27. The Westinghouse Electric Corporation granted $200,000 to the University
of Pittsburgh.

1949   March 26. The Pittsburgh Post-Gazette began

its Sunday edition.

November 8. Mayor Lawrence was reelected.

November 18. The Sunday edition of the
Post-Gazette was sold to the Sun-Telegraph.
Its publication was to be suspended.

1950   The population was 676,806.

April 10. The Marine Hospital was turned
over to the city.

1951   February 7. City Council President Thomas
E. Kilgallen, Controller Edward P. Frey, and
five aides were indicted on a charge of de-
frauding the city of labor and material, and
using it for themselves.

June 17. Mayor Lawrence, and officials of
the Broadway Maintenance Corporation were
indicted on charges of misdemeanors, bribery
and fraud. It was urged that the company's
three million, five hundred thousand dollar
street lighting contract be ended.

October 5. Mayor Lawrence was cleared in
the Broadway Maintenance Corporation case.

October 20. The Pittsburgh Carrier raised
its price to twenty cents.

December 8. The University of Pittsburgh
received $300,000 from the Mellon Education
Trust for scholarships.

1952   January 17. Dutch Premier William Drees
visited Pittsburgh.

August 11. Police Superintendent Harvey J.
Scott was ousted after his involvement in a
brawl.

1953   April 16. The Pittsburgh American League
Hockey team was defeated by Cleveland in
the playoffs.

November 3. Mayor Lawrence was reelected.

1954   January 18. Three Mellon family foundations
gave fifteen million dollars to the University of Pittsburgh Medical School. President
Dwight D. Eisenhower, and University Chan-

cellor Dr. Rufus H. Fitzgerald hailed the
gift.

July 18. Mayor Lawrence visited Israel, and
was made an honorary citizen of Jerusalem.
He presented an honorary scroll from Pittsburgh citizens to Israeli Minister Levi
Eshkol.

1955   October 30. A strike was averted on the
transit system, when the company made an offer to the Motor Coach Union, which was satisfactory to the men.

November 5. The Motor Coach Union accepted
the contract offering a four cents an hour
increase, and an additional one cent in May.
In addition, Mayor Lawrence's proposal for
retroactive pay was accepted.

1956   June 11. A Pittsburgh Hilton Hotel was
planned for the Gateway Center Development.

October 27. The University of Pittsburgh received an anonymous corporate gift of
$500,000 for its health schools building
fund.

1957   November 5. Mayor Lawrence was reelected.

1958   November 4. Mayor Lawrence was elected Governor of Pennsylvania.

Thomas J. Gallagher was elected Mayor.

November 27. The Pittsburgh bicentennial
celebrations got under way.

December 16. The Mellon Education and Chari-
table Trust gave twelve million dollars to
the University of Pittsburgh for the humanities, social sciences and natural sciences.
Chancellor Litchfield said that professor-
ships and fellowships would be named for
the late Andrew W. Mellon.

1959   September 23. Premier Nikita Khrushchev
received the key to the city.

November 4. Joseph Barr was elected Mayor.
He served from December 2 until January 4,
1970.

December 8. The Motor Coach Union trolley
and bus drivers struck for higher pay.

December 13. The trolley and bus operators
accepted a twenty-six cents per hour pay
raise over a three-year period.

1960   The population was 604,332.

April 22. The Pittsburgh Post-Gazette bought
the Sun-Telegraph. . The new paper to be published would be called the Pittsburgh Post-
Gazette and Sun-Telegraph.

June 28. The American Landscape Architects
Society presented an award for the Golden
Triangle project.

September 25. The Pittsburgh Pirates won
the National League Pennant.

October 13. The Pirates defeated the New
York Yankees 10-9 in the seventh game of the
World Series, and thus won the Championship.

October 18. Councilman Homer Greene suspended Assistant Superintendent of Property C.
Raymond Lappe and Contractor Lawrence Martin,
who were indicted for cheating the city of
nearly $11,000.

1961   March 25. The Mayoralty primary date passed,
and the Republican Party was unable to find
a candidate. W. J. Crehan ran without Republican backing against Mayor Barr.

May 19. After the city had refused G. David
Thompson's offer of his modern art collection,
it was sold to a Swiss dealer for between
six and seven million dollars.

November 7. Mayor Barr was reelected.

November 9. It was announced that the Post-
Gazette would drop its Sunday edition.

1962   March 5. Mayor Barr was named Democratic
campaign chairman for the state.

1963   June 14. Thirteen Negro leaders picketed the
site of a new Federal building in Pittsburgh,
to get more skilled blacks into the Unions.

June 29. Announcement was made of the development of a new two hundred and fifty million dollar Panther Hollow Research Center.

1964   April 11. William N. Berger won an international competition for the design of a public
square in the Allegheny Center Renewal Project.

December 18. Assistant Police Superintendent
Lawrence J. Maloney was indicted for income
tax evasion, and suspended.

1965   June 7. Robert Sargent Shriver, Jr. announced that Southern black students at Carnegie Technical Institute would aid in the
anti-poverty war.

July 1. Assistant Police Superintendent
Maloney was dismissed.

August 18. Eleven civil rights pickets were
arrested at the Civic Arena.

November 3. Mayor Barr was reelected.

November 27. The Pittsburgh Board of Education announced that it would transfer eight
hundred and eighty-eight high school pupils
on a voluntary basis to curb racial imbalance, after various civil rights demonstrations protested against overcrowding at mainly black public schools. Busing was rejected as a solution.

1966   January 21. Pittsburgh received a $464,680
Federal grant for beautification.

May 21. About one hundred NAACP demonstra-
tors picketed the Pittsburgh Board of Education protesting alleged racial imbalance in
the public schools.

July 2. The Pittsburgh _Press_ raised its
price from seven to ten cents.

December 17. Mayor Barr asked the Allegheny
County Commissioners to consider giving greater financial support to the City, to cover
those services used by suburbanites. The Mayor indicated that the nonresidents paid only
a ten dollar occupation tax. The county re-
sponded that it would consider this request.

1967   April 6. Six patrolmen, and two ex-patrolmen
            were charged with bribery and extortion, by
            allowing racketeers to operate without any
            opposition.

            September 5. Rev. Alan Walbridge led a de-
            monstration of parents of forty-six white pu-
            pils, who refused to let their children at-
            tend the newly opened Columbia High School,
            where the Board of Education was trying to
            achieve racial balance through busing.

            November 27. Seven of the eight present and
            former patrolmen charged with bribery and ex-
            tortion were cleared of conspiracy charges,
            in which it was claimed they extorted money
            from numbers writers. The suspended men were
            to be reinstated.

1968   April 5. Widespread vandalism broke out af-
            ter the murder of Rev. Dr. Martin Luther
            King, Jr. in Memphis, Tennessee.

            April 7. Governor Raymond P. Shafer ordered
            two thousand two hundred National Guardsmen,
            and three hundred state policemen into the
            Negro Hill district to stop widespread loot-
            ing and damage by black gangs. The Governor
            declared a state of emergency, and banned
            gasoline sales except directly into tanks of
            cars and trucks. He also closed liquor
            stores.

            April 8. Mayor Barr met with Governor Sha-
            fer. They reached an agreement whereby one
            thousand more guardsmen were sent into the
            city.

            April 11. Governor Shafer ordered the with-
            drawal of National Guardsmen.

            June 8. The Catholic Interracial Council
            urged the Human Relations Commission to be
            more aggressive in the race relations field.
            It claimed that the Human Relations Commis-
            sion had failed to develop a campaign among
            Catholics for creation of an understanding
            with blacks.

            June 22. A group of youths, mainly black,
            smashed windows, and looted in the downtown
            section. The police dispersed them with no
            arrests.

June 22. The Pittsburgh Presbytery announced plans for a million dollar neighborhood development and slum improvement program.

October 9. The city refused to sanction vigilante street patrols in the black Homewood-Brushton section, where tensions were high following the killing of a white grocer by two black youths. Clashes had occurred between whites and blacks.

November 16. Theodore W. Kheel was appointed to a mediation panel, which awarded pay increases to the firemen and police.

1969   May 10. The Pittsburgh Steelers, along with the Baltimore Colts and the Cleveland Browns agreed to shift to the American Football League, thus clearing the way for the formation of a single league with two conferences, American and National, containing thirteen teams each.

June 7. The Westinghouse Electric Corporation opened a manufacturing plant in the Homewood-Brushton district, where the 1968 disorders had occurred. It was part of the company program to aid the disadvantaged to become productive and self-sufficient.

June 28. Mayor Barr indicated the serious frustrations of coping with urban problems, and his intent to step down.

November 4. Peter F. Flaherty, an independent who won the Democratic mayoral nomination in the primary on May 21, was elected Mayor by a large majority. This indicated opposition to the regular Democratic organization.

November 29. A major phase in the revitalization of the downtown area was completed with the tenth and final building in the Gateway Center renewal project.

1970   The population was 520,117.

January 5. Mayor Flaherty was inaugurated in the first public inauguration in thirty-six years. He pledged to introduce a reform program.

April 18. Mayor Flaherty's reform program, including dismissal of almost three hundred city employees, brought about a great deal of discussion in the City Council, and upset political alliances and machines.

April 25. Plans were announced for the largest land development project in the city. It would be called Man Plaza.

September 27. The Pirates won the Eastern division National League baseball championship.

October 5. The Cincinnati Reds defeated the Pirates, three games to none, and won the National League Pennant.

August 1. A fight involving black and white policemen at the annual Fraternal Order of Police picnic, increased racial tension, and resulted in a request for a probe of conditions by the Justice Department. Sixty-five members of the Guardians of Greater Pittsburgh, mainly black, withdrew from the organization because of the disturbance.

December 14. Councilman Louis Moran, Jr. was elected the first black City Council President by his fellow members.

December 26. It was announced that since Mayor Flaherty had recently refused to be photographed while accepting a one million dollar check from the Port Authority for removing street car tracks, the Authority had decided to keep the money until the December 31 deadline, depriving the city of $150 per day in interest.

1971   January 4. The municipal service employees went out on strike.

January 9. A tentative agreement by the teachers indicates the first break in the municipal strikes.

January 14. The municipal employees returned to work under a court order.

February 13. The deaths of two firemen in a six-alarm fire reopened the controversy between the firemen's union and the city ad-

ministration concerning the strength of the
fire department. Mayor Peter F. Flaherty
maintained that the reorganization of the Department including phasing out of some fire
companies was not the cause of the deaths.

September 22. The Pittsburgh Pirates won
the National League Eastern Division Title.

October 6. The Pirates defeated the San
Francisco Giants three games to one and won
the National League Pennant.

October 17. The Pirates defeated the Baltimore Orioles to win the World Series, four
games to three.

1972   September 21. The Pittsburgh Pirates won
the National League Eastern Division Championship.

October 11. The Cincinnati Reds defeated
the Pirates three games to two and won the
National League Pennant.

1973   May 15. Mayor Peter Flaherty won the primary election, making it certain that he
would be reelected without opposition in the
November election. He defeated Democrat
Richard S. Caliguri and also won the Republican nomination, having beaten Thomas A. Li-
vingston, a registered Democrat, who was en-
dorsed by the Republican city committee when
no Republicans chose to run.

November 6. Mayor Peter Flaherty was elected
to a second four-year term in an election
that drew the fewest voters in recent city
elections.

1974   January 7. The U. S. Supreme Court agreed to
review the decision which declared a 20% city
tax on private parking operators unconstitu-
tional because it was confiscatory and enacted by the city government which operated
parking facilities.

June 10. The U. S. Supreme Court ruled unanimously that cities may levy taxes on private parking facilities in downtown areas with
high traffic congestion. This involved concern with the need to save urban centers. The
Court indicated that an auto use tax and high

tolls might be fairer than the heavy taxation of parking facilities.

September. The Pirates won the National
League Division Title.

October 9. The Los Angeles Dodgers defeated
the Pirates three games to one and won the
National League Pennant.

1975   May 4. Mayor Peter F. Flaherty joined an
early morning radio program on Station KQB
in addition to his regular duties as mayor.

June 27. Truckdrivers went on strike, stop-
ping the delivery of the Pittsburgh _Press_
and _Post_ _Gazette_. The Pittsburgh Press Company was denied a court injunction to bring
the truckers back to work. The papers had
to stop publication.

July 28. The teamsters' strike ended, thus
enabling the _Press_ and _Post_ _Gazette_ to re-
sume publication.

September 22. The Pirates won the National
League Eastern Division Title.

September 27. The Pittsburgh _Press_ announced
that it was raising its price from 15 cents
to 20 cents as of September 29.

October 7. The Cincinnati Reds defeated the
Pirates three games to none, thus winning the
National League Pennant.

November 30. The public school teachers rejected a last minute contract offer of a
one thousand dollar raise effective the following September.

December 1. The public school teachers voted
to strike over the issue of pay.

1976   January 3. Common Pleas Court Judge Donald
E. Ziegler of Allegheny County ordered the
striking teachers to return to work on
January 5.

January 5. The Board of Education asked the
court to fine the striking teachers union
$25,000 and $1,000 daily for each day that
it continued its walkout. In addition a

daily $100 fine was requested for each mem-
ber of the negotiating team. The Board
cancelled classes indefinitely on January 6.
Judge Donald E. Ziegler fined the Pittsburgh
Federation of Teachers $25,000 on January
12 because they had failed to obey a return-
to-work order.

January 21. The striking school teachers
formally agreed to the general terms of a
ten million dollar salary proposal. They
maintained that they would not end their
seven-week strike until all issues were resolved. These included class size, job security, reading programs, and discipline.
The new contract was ratified on January 26,
thus ending the eight-week strike.

May 6. Mayor Peter Flaherty indicated that
he would not run for a third term.

DOCUMENTS

The documents in this section have been carefully
selected to illustrate the social, political, commercial
and cultural life of Pittsburgh, and its strategic position at the confluence of the Allegheny and Monongahela
Rivers, which aided it in contributing to the trade of
the nation. The most pertinent items from the ordinances, charters and reports of various agencies and departments of the city have been chosen in order to indicate the major changes which have occurred in the government of Pittsburgh. Of great importance is the postwar urban redevelopment program centering around the
Point, and in the area which was the center of Allegheny
before it was annexed to Pittsburgh. Descriptions of
some of the important reconstruction projects are included. Obviously much more could have been included,
but the most important documents were selected due to the
limited space.

PITTSBURGH IN 1761

James Kenny who ran a trading store
at Fort Pitt presented several descriptions of the developing town
and its relations with the Indians
during 1761.

Source: George H. Thurston. Pittsburgh and Allegheny in
the Centennial Year. Pittsburgh, 1876, 6.

11th mo: 19th.--The Fort Banks here is very much
raised, which makes it look much stronger than it was in
times of more danger; by accounts ye front next ye in-
habitanty being of brick, and corners of ye angle of
hewn stone, about--feet high, ye back part next ye point
where ye two rivers meets being of earth and sodded all
so that it grows thick of long grass, that was done last
year, and they have mowed ye bank several times this summer; it's four squair with a row of barracks along each
squair, three rows of which are wooden frame work, and
ye row on ye back side next ye point is brick; also a
large brick house built this summer in ye south east corner, ye roof now aputing on, having fine steps at ye door
of hewn freestone, a cellar all under it; at ye back of
ye barracks opens ye doors of ye magazines, vaults and
dungeons: lying under ye great banks of earth thrown out
of ye great trenches, all round in there are kept ye
stores of ammunition, etc., and prisoners that are to be
tried for their lives; in these vaults there is no light,
but do they carry lanterns, and on ye south east bastion
stands a high poal like a mast and a top mast to hoist ye
flag on, which is hoisted on every first day of ye week
for about eleven to one o'clock, and on state days, etc.;
there are three wells of water walled in ye fort, and a
squair of clear ground in ye inside of about two acres.

20th.-- I have been informed by a young man that
was ordered by ye commanding officer, Collonel Boquet,
(this summer), to number all ye dwelling houses without
ye fort, marking ye number on each door; but there was
above one hundred houses, by ye highest number I have
seen, by better accounts, there is one hundred and fifty
houses, to take notice of which I think was seventy-
eight, these being ye inhabitants of Pittsburg, where two
years ago I have seen all ye houses that were without ye
little fort, they had then thrown down, only one, which
stands yet, also two that was within that little fort is
now standing, being ye hospital now, all ye rest being
built since. which if ye place continue to increase near

this manner, it must soon be very large, which seems
likely to me.

12 mo: 4.-- Many of ye inhabitants have hired a
schoolmaster and subscribed about sixty pounds for this
year for him, he has now about twenty scholars, likewise,
ye soberer part of people seem to long for some public
way of worship, so ye schoolmaster, ect. reads ye Litany
and Common Prayer on ye first day to a Congregation of
different principles (he being a Prisbiterant,) where
they behave very grave, (as I hear) on ye occasion, ye
children are brought to Church as they call it. . . .

12 mo: 25th.-- A young Indian man brought us four
turkeys, saying that he was recommended by several of
his acquaintances to come to ye Quaker who would use
him very well, and having bought them and paid him six
shillings cash, besides victuals and drink, he going out
heard of a better market, so came back and got ye turkeys, delivering ye money again, but his second Chap not
pleased him in dealing, he brought them back to us and
had his money again, but he said Dam it several times
at ye second chap.

BRACKENRIDGE'S ACCOUNT OF PITTSBURGH IN 1786

Hugh Henry Brackenridge who had
come to Pennsylvania with his family in 1753 when he was five years
of age, went to Princeton University, eventually becoming a lawyer,
and settled in Pittsburgh. He was
to become a prominent citizen and
took a moderate and somewhat un-
popular part in the Whiskey Insur-
rection. He eventually was appointed Associate Justice of the
Supreme Court of Pennsylvania.
His description of Pittsburgh in
1786 illustrates the importance of
the Allegheny to the trade and development of the city, and presents an interesting picture of
the surroundings.

Source: "Brackenridge's Account of Pittsburgh in 1786"
in Monthly Bulletin of the Carnegie Library of Pittsburgh, vol. 7, No. 8, October, 1902, pp. 258-262, No. 9,
November, 1902, pp. 288-290, No. 10, December, 1902,
pp. 332-335.

Extract from the Pittsburgh Gazette of July 29, 1786

ON THE SITUATION OF THE TOWN OF PITTSBURGH,
AND THE STATE OF SOCIETY AT THAT PLACE.

The Alleghany River running from the north-east,
and the Monongahela from the south-west meet at an angle
of about 33 degrees, and form the Ohio. This name is
said to signify, in some of the Indian languages, bloody;
so that the Ohio River may be translated the River of
Blood. The French have called it La Belle Riviere, that
is, the Beautiful or Fair River, but this is not intended
by them as having any relation to the name Ohio.
It may have received the name of Ohio about the beginning of the present century, when the Six Nations made
war upon their fellow savages in these territories and
subjugated several tribes.
The word Monongahela is said to signify, in some of
the Indian languages the Falling-in-Banks, that is, the
stream of the Falling-in, or Mouldering Banks.
At the distance of about four or five hundred yards
from the head of the Ohio is a small island lying to the
north-west side of the river, at the distance of about 70

yards from the shore. It is covered with wood, and at the
lower part, is a lofty hill famous for the number of wild
turkies which inhabit it. The island is not more in
length than one quarter of a mile, and in breadth about
100 yards. A small space on the upper end is cleared
and overgrown with grass. The savages had cleared it
during the late war; a party of them attached to the United States having placed their wigwams and raised corn
there. The Ohio, at the distance of about one mile from
its source, winds round the lower end of the island and
disappears. I call the confluence of the Alleghany and
Monongahela the source of the Ohio. . . .
In this rive, at the distance of about one mile above the
town of Pittsburgh is a beautiful little island, which,
if there are river gods and nymphs, they may be supposed
to haunt. At the upper end of the island and towards the
western shore is a small ripple, as it is called, where
the water, bubling as if it sprung from the pebbles of
a fountain, gives vivacity and an air of cheerfulness to
the scene. . . .
     There is a rock known by the name of M'Kee's rock,
at the distance of about three miles below the head of
the Ohio. It is the end of a promontory, where the river bends to the N. W. and where, by the rushing of the
floods, the earth has been cut away during several ages;
so that now the huge overhanging rocks appear, hollowed
beneath, so as to form a dome of majesty and grandeur,
near one hundred feet in height. Here are the names of
French and British officers engraved, who in the former
times, in parties of pleasure, had visited this place.
The town of Pittsburgh, at the head of the Ohio, is
scarcely visible from hence, by means of an intervening
island, the lower end of which is nearly opposite the
rocks.. . . As you ascend the river from these rocks to
the town of Pittsburgh, you pass by on your right hand
the mouth of a brook known by the name of the Saw-mill
run. This empties itself about half a mile below the
town, and is overlooked by a building on its banks, by
the beams of the rising sun. At a small distance from
its mouth is a saw-mill about twenty perches below the
situation of an old mill built by the British, the remains of some parts of which are yet seen.
     At the head of the Ohio stands the town of Pitts-
burgh, on an angular piece of ground, the two rivers forming the two sides of the angle. Just at the point,
stood, when I first came to this country, a tree, leaning
against which I have often overlooked the wave, or commit-
ting my garments to its shade have bathed in the trans-
parent tide. How have I regretted its undeserved fate
when the surly winters flood tore it from the roots and
left the bank bare.
     On this point stood the old French fort known by
the name of Fort Du Quesne, which was evacuated and blown

up by the French in the campaign of the British under
general Forbes. The appearance of the ditch and mound,
with the salient angles and bastions still remains, so
as to prevent that perfect level of the ground which
otherwise would exist. It had been long overgrown with
the finest verdure, and depastured on by cattle; but
since the town has been laid out it has been enclosed,
and buildings are erected.

Just above these works is the present garrison,
built by general Stanwix, and is said to have cost the
crown of Britain 60,0001. Be that as it may, it has been
a work of great labour and of little use--For, situated
on a plain, it is commanded by heights and rising grounds
on every side, and some of them at less than the distance
of a mile. The fortification is regular, constructed according to the rules of art, and about three years ago
put into good repair by general Irwin who commanded at
this post. It has the advantage of an excellent magazine, built of stone; but the time is come, and it
is hoped will not again return, when the use of this
garrison is at an end. There is a line of posts below it on the Ohio river, to the distance of three
hundred miles. The savages come to this place, for
trade, not for war; and any future contest that we
shall have with them, will be on the heads of the
more northern rivers that fall into the Mississippi....

On the margin of this river once stood a row of
houses, elegant and neat, and not unworthy of the European taste, but have been swept away in the course of
time, some for the purpose of forming an opening to the
river from the garrison, that the artillery might in-
commode the enemy approaching and deprived of shelter;
some torn away by the fury of the rising river, indignant
of too near a pressure on its banks. These buildings
were the receptacles of the ancient Indian trade, which,
coming from the westward, centred in this quarter: But
of these buildings, like decayed monuments of grandeur,
not a trace remains. Those who, twenty years ago, saw
the flourish, can only say, here they stood. . . .

On the west side of the Alleghany river, and opposite the orchard, is a level of three thousand acres,
reserved by the state to be laid out in lots for the purpose of a town. A small stream at right angles to the
river, passes through it. On this ground it is supposed
a town may stand; but on all hands it is excluded from
the praise of being a situation so convenient as on the
side of the river, where the present town is placed; yet
it is a most delightful grove of oak, cherry and walnut
trees; but we return and take a view of the Monongahela
on the southern side of the town.

This bank is closely set with buildings for the distance of near half a mile, and behind this range the town
chiefly lies, falling back on the plains between the two

rivers. To the eastward is Grant's Hill, a beautiful
rising ground, discovering marks of antient cultivation;
the forest having long ago withdrawn, and shewn the head
and brow beset with green and flowers. From this hill
two chrystal fountains issue, which in the heat of summer continue with a lympid current to refresh the taste.
It is pleasant to celebrate a festival on the summit of
this ground. In the year 1781 a bower had been erected
covered with green shrubs. . . .

The town of Pittsburgh, as at present built, stands
chiefly on what is called the Third bank; that is the
third rising of ground above the Alleghany water. For
there is the first bank which confines the river at the
present time; and about three hundred feet removed is a
second, like the falling of a garden; then a third, at
the distance of about three hundred yards; and lastly,
a fourth bank, all of easy inclination, and parallel with
the Alleghany river. These banks would seem in success-
ive periods to have been the margin of the river which
gradually has changed its course, and has been thrown
from one descent to another, to the present bed where it
lies. In digging wells the kind of stones are found
which we observe in the Alleghany current, worn smooth
by the attrition of the water. Shells also intermixed
with these are thrown out. Nature therefore, or the river, seems to have formed the bed of this town as a garden with level walks, and fallings of the ground. Hence
the advantage of descending gardens on these banks, which
art elsewhere endeavours, with the greatest industry to
form. Nor is the soil less happy than the situation.
The mould is light and rich. The finest gardens in the
known world may be formed here.

The town consists at present of about an hundred
dwelling houses, with buildings appurtenant. More are
daily added, and for some time past it has improved with
an equal but continual pace. The inhabitants, children,
men and women are about fifteen hundred; this number
doubling almost every year from the accession of people
from abroad, and from those born in the town. As I pass
along, I may remark that this new country is in general
highly prolific; whether it is that the vegetable air, if
I may so express it, constantly perfumed with aromatic
flavor, and impregnated with salts drawn from the fresh
soil, is more favorable to the production of men and o-
ther animals than decayed grounds.
                    * * *

ESTABLISHMENT OF SCHOOLS, 1786-1801

The following advertisements taken
from the Pittsburgh newspapers indicate the types of schools, their
curricula and tuition charges.

Source: Sarah H. Killikelly. The History of Pittsburgh,
Its Rise and Progress. Pittsburgh, 1906., pp. 270-273.

"A Boarding and Day School for Young Ladies,

Will be opened on Wednesday, the fifteenth instant, by
Mrs. Pride, in the house where John Gibson formerly
lived, behind his stone house, where there will be taught
the following branches of needle-work, namely, plain
work, colored work, flowering, lace, both by the bobin
and the needle, fringing, Dresden, tabouring and embroi-
dering. Also reading, English, and knitting if required.
Mrs. Pride from the long experience she has had as a
teacher and from the liberal encouragement she has met
with hitherto both in Britain and in Philadelphia flat-
ters herself that by the utmost attention in teaching the
said branches as also taking the strictest care to the
morals and good breeding of the young ladies placed under
her care that upon trial she will also merit the approbation and encouragement of the inhabitants on this side
the Allegheny mountains."

* * *

"Evening Tuition.

"For the convenience and advantage of such as cannot attend to instructions in the public day school, Mr.
McDonald, by desire, proposes opening an evening school,
in which will be taught Arithmetic, in its various applications to business or the Sciences, bookkeeping, men-
suration and geography, writing in its several sizes and
proportions, the English language correctly and gramma-
tically.
"It is expected the tuition will commence on Monday evening, the 15th of October inst. Applications will
be received at Mr. Jonathan Plummer's, or at Mr. McDonald's school room.
"Pittsburgh Gazette, October twelve, 1798."

* * *

Night School

on Wednesday, the 14th of October next, in one of the
rooms of the Academy, where he means to teach writing,
arithmetic and geometry. Any person who has made a
tolerable proficiency in mathematicks, if his curiosity
prompts him, may, in the course of one quarter, learn
the whole process of making an Almanack.
                                          "John Taylor
    "September twenty-nine, 1801."

                        * * *

                   "Education.

    "The subscriber, being about to leave the Pitts-
burgh Academy, intends to open a school in his house in
Second street, on the 5th of January next, for the re-
ception of a limited number of pupils, to be instructed
in the Latin and Greek languages, writing, arithmetic,
elements of geometry, geography, etc. He will have
frequent examinations, considering them best calculated
to bring into operation two powerful incentives to application, the love of praise, and the dread of dis-
grace. On such occasions the attendance of parents,
guardians and men of education will be requested. He
looks for no patronage but that to which his attention
to the improvement of his pupils in literature and morals will entitle him.
    "Tuition in Latin and Greek $4.00 a quarter.
                                          "Robert Steele
    "December twenty-three, 1802."

PETITION TO ERECT ALLEGHENY COUNTY,
February 15, 1787

The peition indicated a desire on
the part of many inhabitants of
Westmoreland and Washington Counties to establish Allegheny County. They were interested in more
effective government in terms of
administration and justice, as well
as advancement in trade.

Source: John N. Boucher, ed. in chief. A Century and a
Half of Pittsburg and Her People. Pittsburgh, 1908,
vol. I, pp. 241-243.

To the Honorable the Representatives of the Freemen
of the Commonwealth of Pennsylvania in General Assembly
met. The Petition of sundry Inhabitants of the Counties
of Westmoreland and Washington
                              Humbly sheweth
That your Petitioners have seen the Bill published for
consideration entitled an Act for erecting part of Westmoreland and Washington Counties into a separate county.
We are pleased to find the Honorable House have given
time to those Inhabitants who wish to be included in the
new County, to make their sentiments and situation known
to the House upon this subject. Your petitioners conceive by the limits specified in the before mentioned
Bill your honors were not so well acquainted with the
situation of the Country adjacent to Pittsburgh as to fix
the bounds which ought to designate the new County with
that precision the importance of the subject requires,
and as we are unanimously of opinion your honors wish to
lay out the County so as to make the same convenient to
the Inhabitants and without injuring either Washington or
Westmoreland Counties. Your petitioners with due submis-
sion beg leave to give your honors information of what we
humbly conceive to be the proper bounds for the new
County, . . .
        /There follows a description of the boundary7
The above described bounds will give general satisfaction
to every Inhabitant in the two Counties, excepting a few
interested persons or those who make it their business
to object to every measure for the publick good, besides
it will be much nigher and more convenient for every person living within the beforementioned bounds to go to
Pittsburgh to courts or to market than to Washington or
Greensborough, having the advantage of diffirent waters
leading to Pittsburgh to transport ourselves and produce.
At the same time we are obliged to attend Courts of

Justice, either as suitors, jurors or witnesses, we can
carry our produce with us, with which we can pay our
court charges and Tavernkeepers Bills, and also procure
such necessaries as we want for the use of our families.
This is a matter of great importance to us who at present
are labouring under many difficulties for the want of
Cash to patent our Lands and pay our Taxes. Your petition humbly conceive that the laying off a county with
respectable bounds will greatly advantage the Inhabitants
of the three Counties, the greater number of Inhabitants
in a County makes the County Town the Richer, this in-
duces persons of wealth to become Citizens, and conse-
quently a greater consumption of produce. Pittsburgh the
Capital of the Western County seems intended by nature
for a place of consequence from its situation at the confluence of two large Rivers that glide through an extensive and fertile Country, this will induce a great number
of persons of trade and business to settle it, it will
also increase the value of all the lands within the reach
of that market, and also bring forward at an earlier
period the Sale of the State lands, and the Settlement
of that part of the County Northward of Pittsburgh. Your
Petitioners humbly conceive that it is in the intention
of your honors to accommodate the Inhabitants of the new
County with such bounds as will make it more convenient
for them to attend the Courts of Justice at Pittsburgh
than at any other place, and we are happy to inform your
honors that every person residing within the beforementioned bounds will find it more convenient to go to
Pittsburgh than to any other place. Your petitioners
beg leave to inform your honors that we do not mean to
dictate to the honble House, when we mention the bounds,
but only as a matter of information, and this we have.
thought incumbent on us as the persons who are immediately concerned in the consequences that are to ensue from
the determination of the House. Your petitioners therefore humbly pray that your honors would be pleased to
enact a law for erecting a part of Westmoreland and a
part of Washington Counties into a separate County upon
the principles of liberality and justice and your Petitioners as in duty bound will pray, &ca.
      Westmoreland, February 15th, 1787.

CHARTER OF THE BOROUGH OF PITTSBURGH
March 5, 1804

The State Assembly chartered Pittsburgh as a borough on March 5, 1804.
Officers provided for are burgesses and a town council. Specific
regulations concerning duties of
the town government were indicated.

Source: A Digest of the Acts of Assembly Relating to,
and the General Ordinances of the City of Pittsburgh
from 1804 to Jan. 1, 1897, . . . Pittsburgh, Pa., pp.
1-5.

To alter an act entitled "An act to erect the town of
Pittsburgh, in the county of Allegheny, into a borough,"
and for other purposes.

Whereas, The inhabitants of the borough of Pittsburgh, in the county of Allegheny, have petitioned for
an alteration in the law for incorporating said borough,
stating that on a fair experiment they have found the
existing law insufficient to promote conveniency, good
order and public utility; therefor,
SECTION 1. Be it enacted, &c., That the said town
of Pittsburgh shall still continue and forever remain a
borough, under the name and title of "The Borough of
Pittsburgh;" the extent and bounds of which shall be the
same as in the original law, . . .
SEC. 2. That the freeholders, housekeepers, and
other inhabitants of said borough, who have resided within the same at least one year immediately preceding the
election, and within that time paid a borough tax, shall
have power on the third Saturday in March next, and on
the same day in every year hereafter, to meet at the
court-house in said borough, and then and there between
the hours of twelve and six o'clock of the same day, e-
lect by ballot one reputable citizen residing therein,
who shall be styled "the burgess" of said borough, and
thirteen reputable citizens to be a town council, and
shall also elect as aforesaid one reputable citizen as
high constable, all of whom shall be freeholders in said
borough; but previous to said election the inhabitants
shall elect three reputable citizens as judges, one as
inspector and two as clerks of the said election, which
shall be regulated and conducted according to the general
election law of this Commonwealth so far as relates to
receiving and counting votes, and who shall be subject to
the same penalties for malpractices as by the said law

is imposed; and the judges, inspectors and clerks, before
they enter upon the duties of their respective offices,
shall take an oath or affirmation before any justice of
the peace of said county to perform the same with fidelity; and after said election shall be closed shall declare
the persons having the greatest number of votes to be
duly elected; and in the case that any two or more can-
didates should have an equal number of votes, the prefer-
ence shall be determined by lot, to be drawn by the three
judges, whereupon duplicate certificates of said election
shall be signed by the said judges, one of which shall
be transmitted to each of the persons elected, and the
other filed among the records of the corporation; and in
case of the death, resignation, removal or refusal to ac-
cept of any of the said offices, the burgess, or in his
absence or inability to act, the first named of the town
council shall issue his precept directed to the high constable requiring him to hold an election in manner aforesaid to supply such vacancy, giving at least ten days'
notice by advertisements set up at four of the most public places in the said borough.

Sec. 3. That from and after the third Saturday in
March next, the burgess and town council duly elected as
aforesaid and their successors shall be one body politic
and corporate in law by the name and style of "The Burgess and town Council of the Borough of Pittsburgh," and
shall have perpetual succession, and the said burgess and
town council aforesaid and their successors shall be
capable in law to have, get, receive, hold and possess
goods and chattels, lands and tenements, rents, liberties, jurisdictions, franchises and hereditaments to them
and their successors in fee simple or otherwise not exceeding the yearly value of five thousand dollars, and
also to give, grant, sell, let and assign the same lands,
tenements, hereditaments and rents, and by the name and
style aforesaid they shall be capable in law to sue in
this Commonwealth, in all manner of actions whatsoever,
and to have and to use one common seal, and the same
from time to time at their will to change and alter until
it shall be otherwise directed by law. The inhabitants
of said borough may hold two fairs every year hereafter,
to continue two days each, commencing on the first Thursday in June and upon the first Thursday in October.

* * *

Sec. 6. That it shall and may be lawful for the
town council to meet as often as occasion may require,
and enact such bylaws and make such rules, regulations
and ordinances as shall be determined by a majority of
them, necessary to promote the peace, good order, benefit
and advantage of said borough, particularly of providing
for the regulation of the market, improving, repairing
and keeping in order the streets, alleys and highways,
ascertaining the depths of vaults, sinks, and pits for

necessary houses, and making permanent rules relative to
the foundations of buildings, party walls and fences.
They shall have power to assess, apportion and appropri-
ate such taxes as shall be determined by a majority of
them necessary for carrying the said rules and ordinances, from time to time, into complete effect, and also to
appoint a town clerk, treasurer, two persons to act as
street and road commissioners, a clerk of the market, and
a collector, annually, and such other officers as may be
deemed necessary from time to time; _Provided_, That no
by-law, rule or ordinance of the said corporation shall
be repugnant to the constitution or laws of the United
States or of this Commonwealth, and that no person shall
be punished for a breach of a by-law or ordinance made as
aforesaid, until three weeks have expired after the pro-
mulgation thereof, by at least four advertisements set up
in the most public places in said borough: _And provided
also_, That no tax shall be laid in any one year on the
valuation of taxable property exceeding half a cent in
the dollar, unless some object of general utility shall
be thought necessary, in which case a majority of the
taxable inhabitants of said borough, by writing under
their hands, shall approve of and certify the same to the
town council, who shall proceed to assess the same
accordingly.

Sec. 7.   That the burgess elected and qualified a-
greeably to this act, is hereby authorized and empowered
to issue his precept, as often as occasion may require,
directed to the collector, commanding him to collect all
taxes assessed, and to the high constable to collect all
fines and forfeitures imposed by this act, or by the ordinances or regulations of the corporation, and the same
to pay over to the treasury; and the said burgess is
hereby authorized to carry into effect all by-laws enacted by the council, and whatever else shall be enjoined
on him for the well ordering and governing said borough.
He shall have jurisdiction in all disputes between the
corporation and individuals arising under the by-laws.

Sec. 8.   That it shall be the duty of the town
clerk to attend all meetings of the council when assembled upon business of the corporation, and perform the
duty of clerk therto, and keep and preserve the common
seal and records of the corporation and be answerable
for the same, and also for the faithful discharge of all
the duties which may be enjoined upon him by virtue of
this act or of the acts of the corporation, whose attest-
ation with the seal of the corporation shall be good evidence of the act or things so certified. . . .

Sec. 13.   That it shall and may be lawful for the
burgess and town council, or a majority of them, by and
with the consent and approbation of a majority of the
taxable inhabitants of the borough, who by writing under
their hands shall approve and certify the same, to author-

ize any person or persons owning lost bounded by the
Allegheny river and Water street, on the Monongahela
river, to build wharves and erect buildings thereon
opposite their respective lots, subject nevertheless to
such rules, regulations and restrictions as the corporation may deem necessary for the construction of wharves
within the limits of the borough: <u>Provided</u>, That such
wharf or wharves shall be so constructed as not to ob-
struct or impede the navigation of said rivers.

    Sec. 14.   That if any person or persons shall
think him, her or themselves aggrieved by anything done
in pursuance of this act, except in what relates to the
imposing and collecting the borough tax, he, she or they
may appeal to the next court of quarter sessions to be
held for the proper county, upon giving security according to law to prosecute his, her or their appeal with
effect, and the court having taken such order therein
as shall seem to them just and reasonable the same shall
be conclusive against all parties. . . .

INCORPORATION OF THE CITY OF PITTSBURGH
March 18, 1816

The city of Pittsburgh was incorporated on March 18, 1816. In
the selection from the Act printed
below the officers, their powers
and duties are indicated.

Source: A Digest of the Acts of Assembly in Relation to,
and the General Ordinances of the City of Pittsburgh
from 1804 to Jan. 1, 1897. . . . Pittsburgh, 1897,
pp. 6-11.

AN ACT

To incorporate the City of Pittsburgh.

SECTION 1. Be it enacted by the Senate and House
of Representatives of the Commonwealth of Pennsylvania
in General Assembly met, and it is hereby enacted by the
authority of the same, That the inhabitants of the borough of Pittsburgh, in the county of Allegheny, as the
same extends and is incorporated, between the rivers
Allegheny and Monongahela, and also to the middle of
each of the said rivers, and as far down the river Ohio
to such point in the same at which two lines one running
down the middle of each of the said two first mentioned
rivers, shall intersect, which is hereby added to and
incorporated with the original boundaries of said borough are hereby constituted a corporation and body politic by the name and style of "The Mayor, Aldermen and
Citizens of Pittsburgh," and by the same name shall have
perpetual succession, and they and their successors by
such name shall at all times forever be able and capable
in law to have, purchase, receive, possess and enjoy
lands, tenements and hereditaments, liberties, franchises and jurisdictions, goods, chattels and effects,
to them and their successors forever or for any other or
less estate, and the same lands, tenements, hereditaments, goods, chattels and effects, by such name to
grant, bargain, sell, alien, convey, mortgage, pledge,
charge and encumber, or demise and dispose of at their
will and pleasure, and by the said name shall be able and
capable in law to sue or be sued, plead and be impleaded,
answer and be answered unto, defend and be defended in
all courts of record and elsewhere, in all manner of
suits, actions, complaints, pleas, causes, matters and
things that to the said city as a body politic and corporate, in law and in fact, shall and may appertain,
and for that purpose shall have and use one common seal,

and the same from time to time may change. alter, deface
and make anew. ○ ○ ○

SEC. 5. That the power of the corporation of the
said city shall be vested in the said select and common
councils, who shall in common councils assembled have
full power and authority to make, ordain, constitute and
establish such and so many laws, ordinances, regulations
and constitutions (provided the same shall not be repugnant to the laws and constitution of the United States
or of this Commonwealth) as shall be necessary or convenient for the government and welfare of the said
city, and the same to enforce, put in use and execution,
by constables and other proper officers(whom they shall
have power to appoint,) and at their pleasure to revoke,
alter and make anew as occasion may require, and shall
have, hold and enjoy in addition to the powers now vested in the borough of Pittsburgh, which are hereby trans-
ferred to and vested in the said councils, all the powers
and authorities now vested by law in the select and common councils of the city of Philadelphia.

SEC. 6. That in order that a knowledge of the said
laws, ordinances, regulations and constitutions may at
all times be had and obtained and the publications thereof at all times be known and ascertained, such and so
many of them as shall not be published in one or more of
the public newspapers published in the said city within
fifteen days from and after their being severally passed,
ordained and established, and also recorded in the office
of recorder of deeds in and for the county of Allegheny
○○○ within thirty days from and after their being so a-
foresaid passed, ordained and established, shall be null
and void, and before any of the said laws, ordinances,
regulations and constitutions shall be so as aforesaid
recorded, the publications thereof respectively with the
times thereof shall be proved by the oath or solemn affirmation of some credible person, which said oath or
affirmation shall be recorded therewith, and at all times
be deemed and taken as sufficient evidence of the time
of such publication.

SEC. 7. That the doors of the respective halls of
the said select and common council shall be open for the
admission of all peaceable and orderly persons who shall
be desirous of being present at the discussion of any by-
laws, ordinances, rules or regulations for the welfare
and good government of the said city.

SEC. 8. That the Governor shall appoint one recorder and twelve aldermen for the said city who shall
hold their offices during good behavior, and shall severally and respectively have all the jurisdictions, powers and authorities of justices of the peace and justices
of oyer and terminer and jail delivery of and for the
said city, and shall act therein accordingly, jointly or
severally, as fully and amply as any justice or justices

of the peace or of oyer and terminer or jail delivery of
or for any county within this Commonwealth, may or can
do in and for such county; and the justices of the peace
at present commissioned in and for the borough of Pittsburgh shall be aldermen of the said city, and the Governor shall appoint such number of aldermen in addition to
the said justices as shall complete the number herein
directed and limited, and in case of vacancy by death,
resignation, removal from the said city or otherwise of
any of the said aldermen, fill up and supply such vacancy
as soon as may be; and the said recorder and aldermen
and every of them, before he enters on the duties of his
said office in pursuance of this act shall take a solemn
oath or affirmation before the president or one of the
associate judges of the common pleas of Allegheny county,
or before the mayor of the said city for the time being,
"well and faithfully to execute and perform the office
of recorder (or alderman, as the case may be) of the
said city."

SEC. 9. That the members of the select and common
councils shall on the second Tuesday in July next and on
the second Tuesday in January yearly thereafter meet together and elect _viva voce_ one of the said aldermen as
mayor of the said city, whose duty (besides that of an
alderman of the said city) shall be to preside in the
mayor's court when present, to promulgate the by-laws,
rules and ordinances of the corporation, and specially
to attend to the due execution and fulfillment of the
same, and who shall be entitled to receive, hold and enjoy all emoluments which by the laws and ordinances of
the corporation may hereafter be annexed and attached to
the office of mayor; and the mayor elect shall take a
solemn oath or affirmation before the president or an
associate judge of the court of common pleas of Allegheny
county or the recorder of the said city for the time
being, "well and faithfully to execute the office of mayor of said city," and shall thereupon enter upon and
perform the duties of the said office without any further
or other commission, and shall continue in office until
a successor shall be duly elected and qualified, and in
case of the death, resignation or removal of the mayor,
or other vacancy in the said office, such vacancy shall
be filled by a new election for the remainder of his term
in office by the said councils within ten days thereafter, and at least five days notice shall be given in the
public newspapers of the city of the time of holding the
same.

SEC. 10. That each and every mayor, recorder and
alderman of the said city who shall misdemean himself in
office, shall be liable to be removed from office in the
same manner that justices of the peace are by the constitution and laws of this Commonwealth removable for mis-
conduct in office by the general assembly.

SEC. 11.   That the said mayor, recorder and aldermen, or any four or more of them (whereof the mayor or
recorder for the time being shall be one) shall have full
power and authority and they are hereby vested with full
power and authority to inquire of, hear, try and determine, agreeably to the laws and constitution of this
Commonwealth, all forgeries, perjuries, larcenies, as-
saults and batteries, riots, routs and unlawful assem-
blies, and all other offenses which have been committed
or shall be committed within the said city, which would
be recognizable in any county court of quarter sessions
of the peace of or for any county within this Commonwealth, had the same offenses or any of them been committed within any such county, and to punish all persons
who shall be convicted of the same offenses or any of
them agreeably to the laws of this Commonwealth, and also
to inquire of, hear, try and determine all offenses which
shall be committed within the said city against any of
the laws, ordinances, regulations or constitutions that
shall be made, ordained and established in pursuance of
this act, and to punish the offender and offenders as by
the said laws, ordinances, regulations or constitutions
shall be prescribed or directed; also to impose fines on
jurymen and others according to law, and levy the same,
and to award process, take recognizances for keeping the
peace, for being of good behaviour, and for appearance
or otherwise, or to commit to prison, as occasion shall
lawfully require, without being accountable to the Commonwealth for any fines or amercements to be imposed for
the said offenses, or any of them, except such as are or
shall be by law made payable into the State treasury for
offenses against this Commonwealth, and generally to do
all such matters and things within the said city, as any
court of quarter sessions of the peace, . . .

DAVID THOMAS'S VIEW OF PITTSBURGH, 1816

> David Thomas presented his views
> of his travels through the western
> country. He indicated the advan-
> tageous position of the city in
> regard to the development of in-
> dustry.

Source: David Thomas. Travels Through the Western Country in the Summer of 1816. . . . Auburn, New York, 1819.

* * *

This city stands on a plain, by a point of land
formed by the juncture of the Allegheny and Monongahela
rivers. Below this point these waters take the name of
Ohio. It is surrounded by high hills, which close the
prospect in every direction, and on viewing this stream
in the exterior of a great continent, we are surprised
that it has worn its way, round so many obstacles to
the ocean.
The streets of Pittsburg are lighted, and conse-
quently the useful order of watchmen is established. My
ears, however, have not become reconciled to the music.
. . .
Pittsburg is laid out to front both rivers, but as
these do not approach at right angles, the streets intersect each other obliquely.
It is not a well built city. The south-west part
is the most compact, but many years must elapse before
it will resemble Philadelphia. Wooden buildings, inter-
spersed with those of brick, mar the beauty of its best
streets; and as few of these are paved, mud, in showery
weather, becomes abundant. A short period, however, will
probably terminate this inconvenience.
* * *
Two cotton factories, one woollen factory, one paper mill, two saw mills and one flour mill, are all moved
by steam in this city and its suburbs across the Monongahela. Four glass factories, two for flint, and two for
green, are very extensive; and the productions of the
former for elegance of workmanship, are scarcely surpassed by European manufacture. It is sent in many directions from this place; one of the proprietors assured
us that Philadelphia receives a part, but the great out-
let is down the Ohio.
The vast advantages that accrue to this place from
its coal will be appreciated, when we consider, that almost every manufacture owes its existence to this article
of fuel. The glass-houses, the furnaces for castings,
the steam engines, and every domestic fire-place, are

supplied from the mines. These are situate near the
tops of the hills, in every direction from the city;
and the vast mass of earth that once buried this plain,
appears to have been removed by the waters. . . .
    The shafts of these mines extend far into the
hills. . . .The citizens are supplied in their yards for
7 or 8 cents a bushel. . . .
    It is said here. . .that the seasons are much cold-
er than formerly. . . .
    Our common fruit trees do well in Pittsburg. The
peach, the plumb, the apple and the cherry abound on the
branches, though the frosts have been very severe. . . .
    . . . The cheapness, the excellence, and the in-
exhaustible quantity of fuel, that await the hand of
Industry on the banks of these waters, offer facilities
to commerce that no other region of our empire exhibits;
and a population distinguished by enterprize and awake
to this subject will doubtless, soon avail themselves of
advantages so beneficently given.

    Provisions of all kinds bring a high price in this
city though the market is fluctuating. Hay, at present
is twenty dollars a ton and oats one dollar per bushel.
Butter varies from twenty-five to seventy-five cents a
pound. . . .

MORRIS BIRBECK'S NOTES ON PITTSBURGH,
May 29 - June 4, 1817

> Morris Birbeck, an English Quaker
> and farmer. left England determined
> to make a new home for himself and
> his family in America. He presented
> an interesting view of the people
> as well as trade and prices at
> Pittsburgh.

Source: "An English Farmer at Pittsburgh in 1817," <u>Month-
ly Bulletin of the Carnegie Library of Pittsburgh</u>. Vol.
7, No. 6, June 1902, pp. 191-195.

<u>May</u> 29 ⟦1817⟧ Surrounded by all that is delight-
ful, in the combination of the hilly woodlands and river
scenery. At the juncture of the Allegheny and Mononghaha-
la, forming by their union the Ohio, stands the "city
of Pittsburg, the Birmingham of America." Here I expected to have been enveloped in clouds of smoke, issuing
from a thousand furnaces, and stunned with the din of
ten thousand hammers.

* * *

At present the manufacturers are under great difficulties, and many are on the eve of suspending their o-
perations, owing to the influx of depreciated fabrics
from Europe.

Pittsburg contains about 7000 inhabitants, and is
a place of great trade, as an entrepot for the merchandize and manufactures supplied by the eastern states, to
the western. The inhabitants of Kentucky, Ohio, Indiana,
and Illinois, are their customers, and continually increasing in their demands upon the merchants and the ar-
tisans of Pittsburg.

Journeymen in various branches--shoe-makers, tail-
ors, &c., earn two dollars-a-day. Many of them are im-
provident and thus they remain journeymen for life. It
is not, however, in absolute intemperance and profligacy,
that they in general waste their surplus earnings; it is
in excursions, or entertainments. Ten dollars spent at
a ball is no rare result of the gallantry of a Pittsburg journeyman. Those who are steady and prudent ad-
vance rapidly. A shoe-maker of <u>my</u> <u>acquaintance</u>, that is
to say, whom I employed, left Ireland, as poor as an
Irish emigrant, four years ago,--staid one year in Philadelphia, then removed hither, and was employed by a master practitioner of the same calling, at twelve dollars
per week--He saved his money, married, paid his master,
who retired on his fortune, three hundred dollars for
his business, and is now in a fair way of retiring too:

as he has a shop well stocked and a thriving trade,
wholesale and retail, with vast profits.

The low Irish, as they are called even here, too
often continue in their old habit of whiskey drinking;
and, as in London, they fill the lowest departments of
labour in the manufactures, or serve the bricklayers,
&c. They are rude and abandoned, with ample means of
comfort and independence: such is the effect of habitual
degradation of character. The low Irish and the freed
negro, stand at nearly the same degree on the moral
scale, being depressed equally by early associations.

June 2. This evening I heard delightful music from
a piano, made in this place, where a few years ago stood
a fort, from which a white man durst not pass, without
a military guard, on account of the Indians, who were
then hostile lords of this region. A few of the people
still reside at no great distance, and haven in a great
measure, settled into the habits and manners of their
new neighbours.

* * *

Pittsburg is a cheap market for horses, generally
rather more so than we found it: travellers from the
east, often quit their horses here, and take the river
for New Orleans, &c.; and on the contrary, those from the
west proceed eastward from this place, in stages. Thus,
there are constantly a number of useful hackneys on sale.
The mode of selling is by auction. The auctioneer rides
the animal through the streets, proclaiming with a loud
voice, the biddings that are made as he passes along,
and when they reach the desired point, or when nobody
bids more, he closes the bargain.

A complete equipment is, in the first place, a
pacing horse, a blanket under the saddle, another upon
it, and a pair of saddle bags, with great-coat and um-
brella strapped behind.

Women of advanced age, often take long journeys in
this manner, without inconvenience. Yesterday I heard
a lady mentioned familiarly (with no mark of admiration)
who is coming from Tennessee, twelve hundred miles to
Pittsburg with an infant; preferring horseback to boating
up the river.

* * *

JOHN PALMER'S VIEW OF PITTSBURGH, 1817

John Palmer toured the United
States and Lower Canada in 1817.
He presents an interesting view
of the terrain, manufacturing
and commerce.

Source: John Palmer. Journal of Travels in the United
States of North America, and in Lower Canada, Performed
in the Year 1817; Containing Particulars Relating to the
Prices of Land and Provisions, Remarks on the Country
and People, . . . London, 1818, 45-51.

(arrived Saturday, June 14, 1817.)

* * *

The City of Pittsburgh, the capital and emporium
of the western country, is finely situate on a small
plain, surrounded by lofty hills, at the juncture of the
rivers Allegheny and Monongahela, and commencement of
the Ohio, 1180 miles from its confluence with the Mississippi, and containing the course down the Mississippi,
2188 miles from New Orleans.
It is laid out in straight streets, forty and fifty feet wide, having foot-walks on each side. Watch-
boxes are placed at convenient distances, and the police
of the city (except in lighting) is well regulated.
From the number of manufactures, and the inhabitants
burning coal, and the buildings have not that clean appearance so conspicuous in most American towns. The
houses are frame and brick, in the principal street
three story high.
Outside of the town, some log houses yet remain.
. . . The manufacturers, carried on in the neighbourhood, out of the borough, employ many hundred people.
The inhabitants are Americans, Irish, and English. The
Americans are most of them of German and Irish descent.
The public buildings are a jail, . . . a court house,
market house, bank, and several churches.
There are many good stores in Pittsburg, and a
great trade is carried on with Philadelphia, Baltimore,
and the States of Pennsylvania, Ohio, Kentucky, &c.;
. . . The inhabitants send up the Allegheny, Monongahela,
and their forks, whiskey, cyder, bacon, apples, iron, and
castings, glass and foreign merchandize; in return they
receive many thousand bushels of salt from Onondaga,
and immense rafts from Alleghany and French creeks. The
quantity of rafts imported into Pittsburg annually is
computed at 4,000,000 feet; average nine dollars per
1000 feet.

The articles sent down the Ohio and Mississippi, are flour, whisky, cyder, peaches, apples, brandy, bar iron and castings, tin and copper wares, glass, cabinet work, mill-stones, grind stones, rails &c. for which they receive by the return of the keel and steamboats, cotton, lead, furs and peltry, hemp, leaf tobacco, salt, &c.

Numbers of manufactures of almost all kinds, are carried on in Pittsburg, and the vicinity. The country is admirably adapted to the purpose, having plenty of water-falls, mountains of coal, and its tributaries, to convey their wares to all parts of the western country.

The manufactures established at Pittsburg, and in the immediate neighbourhood in 1811, according to Cramer, Spear, and Eichbaum's navigator, printed and published by them were as follows:

one steam flour mill, four stories high, two pair of stones; her steam power calculated for three pair of stones. One cotton manufactury, having a mule of 120 threads, 4 looms, and a wool-carding machine under the same roof. One cotton manufactury, having 234 spindles in operation, turned by horse power. Three glass works, one glass cutter and chandelier manufactury; the articles manufactured are excellent. President Munro's house is furnished with chandeliers, & c. from this establishment.

Three breweries, three distilleries, two air furnaces, two steam engine manufacturies, four nail factories (one of these make 100 ton of cut and hammered nails per annum), seven copper smiths, tinplate workers, and japammers, one wine weaving and riddle manufactury, one brass foundery, six sadlers and harness makers, two gun smiths, three tobacconists, four tallow chandlers, one bell maker, one brush maker, one trunk maker, five coopers, three wheelwrights, one pump maker, two potteries (common), six hatters, one turner, one delft pottery, seven cabinet makers, one comb maker, one spinning wheel maker, four plane makers, thirteen small weavers, ten blue dyers, eight boot builders, seven tan yards, two rope walks, one marble paper maker, one cutler, twenty-one boot and shoemakers, five chair makers, one skin dresser, one button factory, six brick makers, four printing offices, one ink powder factory, one white lead manufactory, one wire drawing steam factory, eighteen blacksmiths, who manufacture all kinds of kitchen and edged tools, and one file and gimblet factory.
            /others are listed/
                * * *

The inhabitants of Pittsburg are fond of music, . . . The houses of the principal streets have benches in front, on which the family and neighbours sit and enjoy the placidity of their summer evenings. . . .

HENRY FEARON'S VIEW OF PITTSBURGH, 1817

Henry Bradshaw Fearon, a London
surgeon, came to America as the
agent of thirty-nine English families to find a part of America
suitable for them to settle.
His "Sketches of America" present
a narrative of his travels throughout the country. His description
of Pittsburgh presents an interesting insight into farming and
industry.

Source: "Extract from Fearon's Sketches of America,"
Monthly Bulletin of the Carnegie Library of Pittsburgh,
Vol. 7, No. 5, May, 1902, pp. 156-159.

PITTSBURGH

Pittsburgh is, in several points of view, a most
interesting town; from its natural situation, being at
the termination of two, and the commencement of a third
river, which has a direct communication with the ocean,
though at the almost incredible distance of 2500 miles;
its scenery, which is truly picturesque; its exhaustless
possession of that first-rate material for manufactories,
coal; its original situation as an early military post,
and remarkable for two defeats of the British, more especially that of General Bradock /sic7 by the French and
Indians, in which the great Washington first distinguished
himself, though but a youth and only a militia colonel,
in covering the retreat of our army; and lastly, its present importance as being the connecting link between
new and old America; and though it is not at present a
"Birmingham," as the natives bombastically call it, yet
it certainly contains the seeds of numerous important
manufactories. The published accounts of this city are
so exaggerated and out of all reason, that strangers are
usually disappointed on visiting it. This, however, was
not my case. I have been in some measure tutored in A-
merican gasconade. When I am told that at a particular
hotel there is handsome accomodation, I expect that they
are one remove from very bad; if "elegant entertainment,"
I anticipate tolerable, if a person is "a clever man,"
that he is not absolutely a fool; and is a manufactory
is the "first in the world," I expect, and have generally
found, about six men and three boys employed.
* * *

FARMING

Agricultural produce finds here a ready and advantageous market. Farming, in this neighbourhood, is not the most profitable mode of employing capital; but it is here, as in all other parts of the Union, an independent mode of life. The farmer must labour hard with his own hands. The "help" which he pays for will be dear, and not of the kind to be relied on, in the mode of its execution, as in England. This may not proceed from a worse state of character, but a <u>difference</u> <u>in</u> <u>condition</u>, as compared with out working class. They are paid about fourteen dollars per month, and board. In many instances they expect to sit down with the master, to live as well, and to be on terms of equality with every branch of the family; and if this should be departed from, the scythe and the sickle will be laid down in the midst of harvest. There is a class of men throughout the western country called "merchants," who, in the summer and autumn months, collect flour, butter, cheese, pork, beef, whiskey, and every species of farming produce, which they send in flats and keelboats to the New Orleans market. The demand created by this trade, added to a large domestic consumption, insures the most remote farmer a certain market. Some of these speculators have made large fortunes.

Land in the neighbourhood of Pittsburgh is worth 100 dollars per acre. At a distance of from five to twenty miles, tracts of from 1 to 500 acres, containing meadow, pasturage, arable, and part covered with wood, have been recently sold at from 20 to 50 dollars per acre. Wheat brings a dollar a bushel; Indian corn, 75 cents a bushel. A four year old cart horse is worth from 20 to 30 dollars; a gig ditto, 50 to 100; a saddle ditto, 20 to 150; a farmer's waggon, 100 dollars; a family ditto, from 50 to 70; cart, 50. An acquaintance of mine, from Derbyshire, gave yesterday for a cow with a calf by her side, twenty-five dollars. Sheep are from one to three dollars;. . . Wool is but little in demand since the termination of the war. Mr.------, of Lexington, has informed me that he purposes making a shipment of it for Liverpool: should this succeed it will open a new source of profit to the western farmer. . . . A brick house, two stories high, containing ten rooms, may be built, with good management, in the country for 4000 dollars..., as the bricks can be made upon the land and the "help" boarded in the house. In towns, a similar building will cost 6000 dollars, exclusive of the ground, which, in particular situations, as of <u>all</u> towns that promise well, is dearer than the most choice spot in the city of London!

COAL

In the coal hills which I have visited, the mineral
is found in a horizontal position, lying at present above
level. It is worked by adits or openings into the side
of the hills, which draw off the water. The stream being
boarded over, the coal is wheeled out in barrows, and
<u>tripped</u> from an overhanging stage into one horse waggons.
The waggons are without wheels, and the horses, if blind,
are preferred, the hills being so steep, that in case of
the least start, nothing can save them from destruction.
Labourers earn in the coal excavations 31s.6d. to 36s.
per week.--If the inhabitants of Pittsburgh are determined to call that place after some English town, I
should purpose that, instead of the "American Birmingham," it be denominated, with relation to the humidity
of its climate, "the American Manchester;" for I remained at this place several days, during which time the
rain never ceased. The smoke is also extreme, giving to
the town and its inhabitants a very sombre aspect; but
an English medical gentleman who has resided here some
years, informs me that there is not a more healthy place
in the United States. The diseases are billious remit-
tent fevers; rheumatic among the aged; <u>a few</u> cases of
bronchocele which affects the theroid /sic/ gland of
females; and inflammatory sore throat in wet weather.
Medical aid is easy of attainment, though not always of
the most valuable kind. There is of doctors, as of
lawyers, too large a supply, and of course many of them
very inefficient. A physician here is also a surgeon--
prepares his own medicines, and practises in every department of the profession;--generally they are neither
so well educated, nor in such respectable circumstances
as our medical men.

TRADES AND MANUFACTORIES.

The manufacturing interest of Pittsburgh is that
of the United States. Many of the manufactories originated during the late war, and all of them flourished
during its continuance. At present they are generally
upon the wane. A document was issued from their committee last year, setting forth their distress in the strong-
est language--from which it would appear to equal that
of our manufacturing classes even during the worst period
of their sufferings.

* * *

INCORPORATION OF THE PITTSBURGH GAS LIGHT
AND COKE COMPANY, December 21, 1827

In order to provide light for the
city, the Pittsburgh Gas Light and
Coke Company was incorporated. Basic regulations concerning its administration and the rights of
shareholders are indicated.

Source: A Digest of the Ordinances of the City of Pittsburgh: To Which is Prefixed a Collection of the Acts of
the Assembly Relating to the Corporation. Pittsburgh,
1849, 62-63.

AN ACT
Incorporating the Pittsburgh Light and Coke Company,
passed the twenty-first day of December, one thousand eight hundred and twenty-seven.

WHEREAS, William R. Griffith has obtained from the
mayor, aldermen and citizens of Pittsburgh, the exclusive privilege of supplying the said city with gas for a
term of years, agreeably to articles of agreement entered into between the said city and William R. Griffith,
bearing date the tenth of August, one thousand eight
hundred and twenty-seven. And for the purpose of carrying the said agreement more fully into effect, and of
supplying such persons with gas as are desirous to use
the same, the said William R. Griffith is willing to
transfer the said agreement to a company to be formed
for that purpose: And whereas, Benjamin Page, Benjamin
Bakewell, James S. Craft, Henry Holdship, and Harmar
Denny, and their associates, subscribing articles of
association for the purpose of forming said company,
have, by their petition, presented to the Legislature,
prayed for an act of incorporation for the purpose a-
foresaid: Therefore,
SECTION I. Be it enacted, That all such persons as
now are or hereafter shall be stockholders of the said
company shall be and they are hereby created a body politic and corporate in fact and in name, by the name and
style of the "Pittsburgh Gas Light and Coke Company;" and
by the said name they and their successors shall and may
have continual succession, and shall be in law capable
of sueing and being sued, pleading and being impleaded,
in all courts and judicatures whatsoever, in all manner
of actions and suits whatsoever; and also of constructing
and being constructed with relative to the funds of the
said corporation, and the business and the purposes for
which the said corporation is created, as hereinafter

declared; and they and their successors may have a common seal, and may change and alter the same at pleasure.

SECT. II. That the corporation hereby created is so
created for the purpose of supplying the said city by the
said William R. Griffith, for the purpose of supplying
the said city with gas light, and such individuals as
may desire a supply of the same, and to distributing and
disposing of gas, coke and other products of distillation
from coal, and to the manufacturing and erecting the necessary apparatus, pipes and other articles necessary for
carrying the same into effect, and to constructing the
proper buildings, and for no other purpose whatsoever,

SECT. III. That the capital stock of the said corporation shall be twenty thousand dollars, which shall be
divided into two hundred shares of one hundred dollars
each; which may be increased to forty thousand dollars,
to be divided into four hundred shares of one hundred
dollars each, with the consent of the subscribers, at a
general meeting, in such manner and on such terms as the
managers may ordain and determine.

SECT. IV. That the stock, property and affairs of
the company shall be conducted by a president and six
managers, to be chosen from among the stockholders, by
ballot, in person or by proxy, on any day within six days
after the passage of this act, who shall hold their offices for one year and until others may be chosen and no
longer; and who shall have the power of appointing the
secretary, treasurer, and other officers required. In
all such elections,

      One share shall be entitled to one vote,
      Three shares, -   -   -   two votes,
      Five shares, -   -   -   three votes,
      Ten shares, -   -   -   - five votes,
And every five shares above ten, one additional
vote.
And no person shall be allowed to vote unless the full
amount of instalments regularly called for are paid, or
until sixty days after the transfer is registered.

SECT. V. That the stock of the said corporation
shall be assignable and transferable according to such
rules as the board of managers may establish, and shall
be considered personal property. Certificates may be
issued or renewed to the several holders of stock, first
being signed by the president and secretary: _Provided_,
That no transfer be made or certificate given until all
debts due or owing to the company shall be first duly
satisfied, and the company shall have the first right to
purchase the shares at the prices offered for them.

SECT. VI. That the board of managers shall have the
power to lease or purchase, in fee simple, such real estate as may be necessary for carrying on the business:
Provided, That same shall not exceed in value ten thousand dollars. They shall declare a dividend twice in

each year of so much of the profits arising from the
stock of the said company as to them shall appear ad-
visable, reserving ten per cent of such profits as a
contingent fund, until such contingent fund amounts to
ten per cent. of the whole capital stock paid in; and
any manager consenting to a larger dividend shall be personally and individually liable for the same to the company. The said managers shall have power to adopt by-
laws shall not be inconsistent with the constitution and
laws of this State and of the United States; fix the
compensation of the officers, and generally to make all
contracts for the said company, which shall be signed by
the president and secretary; to hold their meetings when-
ever requisite; four of said managers being competent to
transact all such business, and no smaller number.

SECT. VII. That a general meeting of the stockholders, for the election of the president and managers,
and for other purposes, shall be held on the second Monday
of February in each year, at which a report shall be made
of the state of the company's affairs, which report, after
adoption, shall be open to the inspection of the stockholders during the hours of business for three months.

. . .

PITTSBURGH IN 1828

Mrs. Ann Royal, editor of "The
Huntress" and "Paul Fry" in Washington, D. C., travelled throughout Pennsylvania in the late
1820's. She visited Pittsburgh
and was impressed by the loca-
tion and planned developemnt.

Source: John N. Boucher, ed. in chief. A Century and a
Half of Pittsburgh and Her People. Pittsburgh, 1908,
vol. I, pp. 351-353.

. . . Of all towns in our country, Pittsburg
excites most astonishment. Everything pursued in other
towns is thrown into the shade in Pittsburg; even in the
building of steamboats it excels, by a long way, our
great city, New York. You see nothing but columns of
smoke rolling out of these manufactories in every part
of the city and in every street. Go to the river Monongahela, and you see nothing but steamboats, two stories
high, many of them, and two tiers of windows, precisely
like a house with gable ends.
     As we drove down the Allegheny river we were close-
ly hemmed in by a vast hill on out left. This hill makes
a sudden stop as you draw near the city, and runs across
in a steep, perpendicular precipice to the Monongahela
river, forming a perfect wall in its rear seventy feet
high. This hill takes different names in its progress;
that part opposite the point or the great body of the
city is called Grant's Hill, so named from Col. Grant,
who was defeated on its summit by the French and Indians
in 1758; that part of it on the Monongahela is called
Boyd's Hill, from one Boyd who hung himself there;
that part extending to the Allegheny river is also distinguished by the name of Quarry Hill, being 440 feet
high. From each river there are also seen vast hills so
that you are in the city before you can see it. Its
situation is much lower that I expected to find it. The
city runs up the banks of both rivers beyond its limits
in the center, running much farther up the Allegheny however. The two rivers and the point give it the form of
a triangle. It is about one mile on the one river and
one and three-quarters on the other. The whole city sits
on an even plain, about 30 to 40 feet above the low water
mark, higher, however, on the Allegheny side. On the
opposite shore of the Monongahela river is another called
Coal Hill. Coal Hill is 465 feet high and very rugged.
The height of Hogback Hill is unknown. It is a barren
eminence of unsightly appearance. In all these eleva-

tions coal is found except on Grant, Boyd and Higback Hills, their altitude not being sufficient to bring them within the range of the great strata of that mineral which pervades the region.

The scenery around Pittsburg is very beautiful, highly delightful in summer and when viewed from some points presents the most interesting association of nature and art. The view from Coal Hill is not surpassed in any country, earth, air, rocks, water, woods, town and sky break upon the vision in forms the most picturesque and delightful. Coal Hill affords another point of interesting observation where the eye at a single glance takes in a hundred beauties that might vie with the purest and brightest of the other hemispheres.

Pittsburg has several suburban villages that contribute to and are supplied from the great center with which their strength and prosperity are intimately connected. On or nearly adjoining the northeastern boundary of the city and on the flat between Quarry Hill and the Allegheny River the Northern Liberties are situated and are intended as a continuation of the city. They were laid out in 1816 by George A. Bayard and James Adams and are now improving rapidly and contain the Phoenix Cotton Factory, the Juniata Iron Works, etc. Adjoining the southeastern boundary of the city on the north stands Kensington, or as it is some times called--Pipetown, deriving its name through one of its early settlers, an eccentric little gentleman still well known among all classes for his odd humor and the universality of his mechanical business, Mr. William Price, who established a pipe manufactory there. Kensington is partly on a steep hill side, the houses, which are low, seem to stick to Boyd's Hill by magic. Over the Monongahela is another considerable village called Birmingham; it is incorporated into a borough and sits at the base of Coal Hill on the bank of the river and here the celebrated Birmingham glass is manufactured. It also contains several steam mills and an extensive lock manufactory. It is well built and makes a handsome appearance from Pittsburg. Over the Allegheny river, directly opposite the city, is another very handsome and flourishing town called Allegheny. The Western Penitentiary is built here, one of the most splendid buildings in the United States and the site of the town is by far one of the most pleasant of any in the vicinity, not excepting Pittsburg itself. It is unrivaled in scenery and soil. There are two superb bridges, one over the Allegheny and one over the Monongahela of the first architecture and are the finest ornaments belonging to Pittsburg.

* * *

I read so much of the steam manufactories and coal and smoke of Pittsburg that I tried to form some idea of them, but was greatly disappointed. More smoke

than I could have conceived, and the manufactories were
far beyond my conception in skill of workmanship and
amount of capital.

Pittsburg City has a population of 10,600, Northern
Liberties 711, Kensington 390, Birmingham 459, Allegheny
711, miscellaneous 260. Of those born in foreign coun-
tries there are 3,000 nearly. Pittsburg at the last e-
numeration contained, dwelling houses 1,140, Churches
12, public buildings 7, stores 60, groceries 146, banks
2, taverns 16, factories, mills and shops 440, ware
houses, etc., 76. This number, however, has greatly increased and the buildings are going up at the same time
in all parts of the city. Most of the houses are brick,
and some of them are lofty, fine buildings, but all of
the houses are colored quite black with the smoke. The
interiors of the houses are still worse. Carpets,
chairs, walls, furniture are all black with smoke; no
such thing as wearing white; the ladies mostly dress
in black and a cap or white ruff put on clean in the
morning is tinged quite black by bed time. The ladies
are continually washing their faces. Many times the
smoke, particularly in the absence of the sun is quite
annoying to the eyes of strangers, and everything has a
very gloomy, doleful appearance at first (excepting always the interior of the work shops). But in a few days
the stranger becomes so familiar to it that the novelty
of the thing is completely worn off and your walks and
rambles through the city are pursued with the same pleasure common to others.

In all the towns of Pennsylvania the public buildings and offices are built on squares in the center of
their towns. These squares are uniformly called the
"Diamond." I had often heard the word but from haste
and inattention never stopped to ask what it meant, and
that it meant the public square is one of the last things
I should take it to apply. . . . The diamond is about
the center of the town, is large and contains the market
house in the center and the public buildings, attorneys'
offices and a few oyster cellars. The public buildings
are large and well built of brick. The churches are
small and make no show except one just rebuilt, touched
off in great gothic style. The streets of Pittsburg are
not regular, running in all directions; most of them,
however, angle with the Monongahela. They are paved but
not lighted. The side walks as a whole are dirty and in
wet weather very muddy in some parts of the town. The
citizens are now engaged in furnishing the city with
good water and have sunk a very handsome reservoir upon
the top of Grant's Hill for the purpose, but for some
cause, to me unknown, the pipes have mostly bursted and
filled the streets with water, which I find very unpleas-
ant.

There are in Pittsburg thirty-two attorneys and

counselors and 16 physicians, a museum, the Western University, a high school, an academy and 40 smaller schools. The manners of the people of Pittsburg, as in all other large towns, some are liberal and polite and others quite the reverse. The University exists only in name and cannot be said to be in operation though it has a long string of professors. Miss Parry is at the head of an academy for young ladies. Misses Roberts and Campbell have a large school of both sexes. The Sisters of Charity also have a very large school. The high school is by far the best conducted seminary in that place. It is kept in the Unitarian Church. The name of the principal is E. Worthington, Esq. He has 54 students.

Lambdin's Museum and gallery of paintings was established September 8, 1828, and now contains a valuable collection of paintings from ancient as well as modern masters. Fine land sketches by Doughty, Birch, Lawrence, etc.; pictures from the collection of Baron Muller, portraits of distinguished characters by Stuart, Sully, Peale and Lambdin. The museum contains about two hundred foreign birds among which are the "Birds of Paradise," 20 quadrupeds, 500 minerals, 300 fossils, 300 marine shells, 1,200 impressions of medals, 100 ancient coins and a handsome collection of articles from the South Seas Marine Protection, Indian articles, etc. Mr. Lambdin is himself an artist and his museum is the one specimen of taste or amusement in the city. No library, no atheneum, no gardens, no theaters. I understand there was an Apprentice's Library gotten up by a few liberal gentlemen, Messrs. Holdship, Eichbaum and several others. There are, however, many liberal and enlightened men in Pittsburg. The whole city is a perfect work shop and the most remarkable fact in regard to the character of the city of Pittsburg, and one that excites astonishment and pleasure, is that the mechanics and artificers are by far the most enlightened part of the city. There is not a more honorable, orderly, well behaved class of men, doubtless, to be found on the globe of their calling.

* * *

PETITION FOR ESTABLISHMENT OF AN
EDUCATIONAL SYSTEM, JANUARY 1831

Various petitions were sent to the
State Legislature requesting that
it provide funds for elementary
education throughout the State.
The appeal printed below was so
eloquently made that the Legislature passed an act on April 2,
1831 to establish a general system of education. This was, however, only the beginning of the
process, because it did not provide for the schools. The act establishing a general system of education by common schools was
passed April 1, 1834 which provided the necessary funds and directions for the school system.

Source: Sarah H. Killikelly. The History of Pittsburgh,
Its Rise and Progress. Pittsburgh, 1906, 309-316.

To the Honorable the Senate and House of Representatives of the Commonwealth of Pennsylvania, The memorial
of the subscribers, citizens of the said Commonwealth.
Respectfully sheweth: That your memorialists contemplate with regret the imperfections of the system of
public education now established in Pennsylvania, and are
desirous that the constitutional provisions on this subject may be carried into effect by adequate Legislative
movements.
We regard the existing laws as insufficient for
that purpose. Their effect has not been that universal
extension of education which the nature of our republican government requires; and there is reason to fear that
if they are continued without improvement, they will
yearly become more defective in their operations.
We lament that a Commonwealth like ours, powerful,
wealthy, distinguished for wise laws and gigantic inter-
nal improvements, should remain inferior to any of her
sister states, in a matter of such vital importance as
the diffusion of education. We earnestly request that
you will, as speedily as possible, direct your attention
to this subject; and establish by law a uniform system
of schools, to be supported at the public expense, in
every district of the State where the inhabitants are
willing to receive them. It is well known that in New
England and the State of New York, the public schools
are so well conducted as to supercede, to a great extent,

the necessity of supporting private establishments and we doubt not that the same might, with proper exertions, be made the case in Pennsylvania.

Resolved, That the proceedings of this meeting be published in all papers of this city.

To the Honorable Senate and House of Representatives of the State of Pennsylvania, the memorial of the subscribers and citizens of the said Commonwealth showeth:

That your memorialists contemplate with regret the imperfections of the system of public education now established in Pennsylvania and are desirous that the constitutional provisions on this subject, established in 1790, viz: 'That the Legislature shall as soon as conveniently may be, provide by law, for the establishmemt of schools throughout the State,' may be carried into effect by the Legislature unanimously. . . .

Your memorialists further beg leave to state that there have already been one hundred and fifty thousand dollars expended by the Legislature for colleges and academies, from which institutions the poor classes have been excluded. This your memorialists believe to be anything else than what the framers of our constitution intended. Happily ignorant of the different grades in society, aware that no one is debarred from our political institutions, we consider it a duty to establish a system of liberal education, as extensive as circumstances can possibly authorize. The details of such a plan are of course left to the wisdom of the Legislature. Your memorialists, however, take the liberty of mentioning that a committee be appointed which shall divide the State into such school districts, in which there may be proper officers, elected by the people to establish and regulate the schools, as directed by the vigilance of those officers that no incompetent or unworthy teacher may find a place therein. Each district may use all or part of its own funds, which would not amount to more than is now expended by individuals for that purpose.

Your memorialists are informed from undoubted authority that while there are at least four hundred thousand children in Pennsylvania, between the ages of five and fifteen, there were not during the past year one hundred and fifty thousand in all the schools of the State, then it is probable that two hundred and fifty thousand children capable of instruction, were not in the schools during the past year. Many of these children never go to school at all. Multitudes are living and continuing to live in ignorance, and multitudes more receive at the best, but the most superficial instruction. We earnestly request that you will, speedily as possible, direct your attention to the subject and establish by law a uniform system of schools to be supported at public expense. . .

ESTABLISHMENT OF FOUR WARDS
January 5, 1836

As Pittsburgh grew in size the Council determined to further divide the
city into four wards: the North,
South, East and West wards. The
boundaries are established in the
ordinance.

Source: A Digest of the Ordinances of the City of Pittsburgh. . . Pittsburgh, 1849, 302-303.

WARDS

AN ORDINANCE

To divide the city into wards or districts, and
for other purposes.

SECTION I. That from and after the passage of this
ordinance, the city of Pittsburgh shall be divided into
four wards, in the manner following, viz:
So much of the said city as lies northwardly of the
middle of Liberty street, and eastwardly of the middle of
Marbury street, shall be one ward to be called the north
ward. So much of the said city as is included in the
following boundaries, viz: beginning at the middle of
Liberty and Marbury streets, and running thence down Marbury street to the Allegheny river, thence along the
Allegheny river to its confluence with the Monongahela
river, thence up the middle of Wood street to the middle
of Diamond alley, thence up the middle of Diamond alley
to the middle of Market street, thence down the middle
of Market street to the middle of Liberty street, and
thence down the middle of Liberty street to the place
of beginning, shall be one ward, to be called the west
ward. And so much of the said city as is included in the
following boundaries, viz: beginning at the foot of
Wood street on the Monongahela river, thence up the middle of Wood street to the middle of Diamond alley, thence
along the middle of Diamond alley to the Farmers and
Mechanics' turnpike road, thence along said road to the
city line, and thence by the same to the Monongahela
river, thence down said river to the place of beginning,
shall be one ward, to be called the south ward. And so
much of the city as lies south of the middle of Liberty
street, east of the middle of Market street, Diamond alley, and the boundaries of the south ward, above named,
shall be one ward, and be called the east ward. . . .
ORDAINED AND ENACTED into a law in Councils, this 5th day
of January, A.D. 1836.

ESTABLISHMENT OF A PERMANENT WATCH
March 26, 1836

As the city grew it became necessary to provide greater police
protection through a night watch.
The ordinance, passed on March 26,
1836, provided for a captain, lieutenant and watchmen as well as explained their duties.

Source: A Digest of the Ordinances of the City of Pittsburgh: To Which is Prefixed a Collection of the Acts of
Assembly Relating to the Corporation. Pittsburgh, 1849,
306-307.

AN ORDINANCE

For the establishment of a permanent watch.

SECT I. /Supplied/
SECT. II. That it shall be the duty of the captain
to repair to the watch house, to be designated from time
to time, before 9 o'clock P.M., of each day, there to remain until the hour appointed for the dismissal of the
watch. . . The said captain of the watch is hereby in-
vested with all the powers and authorities of the high
constable, all the duties of said officer being likewise imposed, except that of registering carriages, car
carts, and drays; and he is furthermore directed to report to the mayor, any negligence, or want of fidelity,
that may have been observed in any of the persons under
his direction, that they may be forthwith fined, or if
expedient, stricken from the roll, as will be hereinafter
pointed out.
SECT. III. That it shall be the duty of the lieutenant of the watch, who is hereby clothed with all the
powers and authorities of the city constables, to attend
at the watch house at 9 o'clock P.M., every night, (unless necessarily absent) to receive instructions; and in
the absence of the captain, the lieutenant shall take
upon himself all the duties of said officer, and be held
accountable for their proper execution. He shall report
himself every two hours through the night, at the watch
house, (unless engaged in some special service by order
of his superior), for the purpose of reporting anything
of importance he may have learned in his rounds from the
watchmen, or from his personal observation, and particularly to report any lack of good faith which he may have
observed in the persons under his supervision.
SECT. IV. That the watchmen selected shall be of

reputable standing, and they are hereby vested with all
the powers and rights of the city constables, as defined
by the act incorporating the city of Pittsburgh.   It shall
likewise be their duty to report themselves at 9 o'clock,
P.M., of each and every night at the watch house, for the
purpose of inspection and instruction; and together with
the captain and lieutenant, at such other times at the
mayor's office as may be considered of importance to the
public peace.   They shall repair to their respective
stations as soon after roll call as possible, and continue
vigilant on the beats appointed for them, until half past
four o'clock, A.M., of each day, from the 21st of March
until the 21st of September, and until six o'clock A.M.,
of each day, from the 21st of September, until the 21st
of March, at which designated hours they shall assemble
at the watch house, and convey any prisoners therein con-
fined to the mayor's office, to be dealt with according
to law.

    SECT. V.   That they are hereby empowered, and re-
quired to apprehend all assassins, robbers and other
violators and disturbers of the public tranquility, or
any and every one, they may have cause to suspect of
any unlawful or evil designs, as well as drunkards and
vagrants, and shall take the person or persons so appre-
hended, as soon as conveniently they may to the public
watch house.   And they are hereby especially required in
time of fire, to alarm each other, the inhabitants in
their immediate neighborhood, and the officers of fire
companies who may reside within their respective sections,
and shall thereupon repair to their several stations,
the better to apprehend any persons, who may be felon-
iously carrying away any of the foods and chattels of
an other. . . .

PITTSBURGH FIRE, April 10, 1845

This fire, one of the worst suffered by Pittsburgh, destroyed
a large part of the city. The
description printed below indicates the extent of the damage,
plans for reconstruction, and aid
give to the city.

Source: Sarah H. Killikelly. The History of Pittsburgh,
Its Rise and Progress. Pittsburgh, 1906, pp. 185-189.

At five minutes past twelve N. on that fatal day,
a fire broke out in an old shed on the east side of
Ferry Street, corner of Second. It is generally be-
lieved now to have originated from a fire built in the
yard adjoining it, by a washerwoman. The weather had been
'parching dry' for two weeks previous to this time, and
high winds had been carrying every particle of moisture
from the buildings of the city, so that they were like
timber prepared for burning. It was in this state of
things that the tocsin sounded -- the bell of the Third
Presbyterian Church was struck.
At the very first, we are assured by an eye wit-
ness, there did not seem to be very much danger. For
half an hour after the fire broke out, the wind, which
had been blowing all morning, slept in a propitious lull.
If there had been plenty of water, it is this gentleman's
opinion that the fire could have been easily put out.
But the water was low in the reservoir, and the first
efforts of the fire engines resulted only in sucking mud;
the water did not come. It was then that the west wind,
waking from the noontide siesta that our spring winds so
often indulge in, arose in his might, and commenced to
fan the incipient flames into a mighty fire. And it was
then that the city woke up to its true danger. As soon
as the wind fairly arose again, the fire started forth on
its destructive course with the rapidity of lightning.
It fairly licked up the dry wooden frames on the west
side of Ferry Street. It leaped across that street in
different directions, but its most serious course was to
the Globe Cotton Factory, opposite. . . . Commencing on
the corner of Ferry and Second Streets it crossed Ferry
and spread out like a fan of flame through the squares to
the eastward and wouthward. After attacking the Globe
Factory it threatened the Third Presbyterian Church, which
was only saved by the tremendous unremitting exertions
of the people; and nobly were those exertions rewarded,
for by saving that church at least a dozen squares of
the city to the northeast were saved also. . . . The

fire. . . progressed diagonally across the square bounded
by Ferry, Third, Market and Second Streets, and about
equally as fast up the entire square bounded by Ferry,
Second, Market and Front Streets. After crossing Market
it extended in one broad wave on one side down to Water
Street, and on the other diagonally up to Diamond Street
on the corner of Wood. This was its greatest width. Between Wood and Smithfield the wave began to recede from
Diamond Street to Fourth; but from Smithfield onward it
swept along, four and a half squares broad, until it
reached Grant Hill and the Canal. Here it skipped over
a number of frame and other buildings in a most unac-
countable way and recommenced devouring everything clear
up to the end of Pipetown, or Kensington, as it was then
called -- a suburb then; integral part of the city now.
There it was arrested by the dearth of food to satisfy
its fierce appetite. There were no more houses in that
direction for it to burn, and the Great Fire of Forty-
five was virtually over. The fire began at noon, and
at seven o'clock in the evening its fury was spent. In
that time it had lain the best oart of the city in ash-
es -- nay in the two hours from 2 to 4 P. M. the greater
part of the immense destruction was wrought, such was the
rapidity of its spread.

    The boundaries of the burnt district may be thus
described: From Water Street up Ferry to Third Street
(the Third Presbyterian Church was saved); up Third to
Wood; up Wood to Diamond Alley; up Diamond Alley to
Smithfield Street, and thence down Smithfield to Fourth
Street; up Fourth to Ross Street, and thence to the head
of Pipetown -- including twenty squares, and comprising
from one thousand to twelve hundred houses, many of the
warehouses containing goods of immense value; they were
grocery, dry goods, and commission houses, and their
stock had been just laid in. The space burned over was
estimated to cover fifty-six acres. Twenty squares in
the heart of the city were utterly destroyed.

    This flourishing suburb, Pipetown, was well nigh
annihilated. The course of the fire was extraordinary.
The last large building in the city this side of it was
the new steel works of Jones and Quigg. When the fire
reached this it dipped down a steep bank into the canal,
and consumed the lock-tender's house, and then rising it
went completely over a number of frame buildings on the
opposite bank, including the workshops of Mr. Tomlinson,
the contractor of the iron steam ship on the stocks,
Parry and Scott's foundry, the Gas Works, the Messrs.
Phillips' glass house and lighting on the glass works of
Messrs. Miller & Co., commenced anew with the utmost fury.
It took everything from thence up on that side of the
road and made a clean sweep of all between the hill and
the river to the utmost end of the town. The greatest
loss was in the Dallas Iron Works. With very few escep-

tions all the inhabitants were operatives in or depen-
dent on the mills, and foundries; and by this calamity
hundreds of them were rendered houseless and homeless.

A committee appointed by the Councils, after a
full examination of the burnt district, arrived at the
following estimate of losses: 982 buildings burnt, valued
at $1,500,000.00; personal property value, $900,000.00;
total, $2,400,000.00. Subsequent estimates of the total
loss to the city ranged from $5,000,000.00 to $8,000,000.
The following public buildings were totally destroyed:
The Firemen's Insurance Office, the Fire and Navigation
Insurance Office, the Penn Insurance Office, the Mayor's
Office, Tombs, Merchants and Board of Trade Reading
Rooms, its files and valuable library, Philo Hall, all
in one building, the Bank of Pittsburgh, the Chronicle
Office, the Merchant's Hotel, Wood Street; the Eagle
Hotel, Third Street; The Monongahela House, the American
Hotel, corner of Third and Smithfield Streets; the Smith-
field Hotel, corner of Third and Smithfield Streets;
the Associate Presbyterian Church, on Fourth Street; the
Baptist Church, corner of Grant and Third Streets; the
Western University, the African Methodist Church, Second
Street; the Scotch Hill Market House; the Monongahela
Bridge and the Custom House.

Relief soon began to pour in from all quarters.
The Legislature appropriated $50,000.00 to meet the
actual necessities of the occasion, and remitted taxes
for State and county purposes and on real estate in the
burnt district, and released the business men from the
payment of mercantile license. Curious to relate, Pittsburgh Councils failed to donate a single cent to the
sufferers. The total contributions from outside sources
slightly exceeded $199,566.00, of which Pennsylvania
contributed $109,890.00; New Hampshire, $329.00; Massa-
chusetts, $16,741.00; New York, $23,265.00; New Jersey,
$557.96; Maryland, $11,513.00; Delaware, $1,322.00;
District of Columbia, $2,872.00; Ohio, $10,081.00; Michi-
gan, $100.00; Kentucky, $5,773.00 Tennessee, $1,259.00;
Indiana, $52.00; Missouri, $3,883.00; Alabama, $1,652.00;
Mississippi, $1,291.00, Georgia, $470.00; Louisiana,
$7,167.00; and Europe, $651.00

Thousands were forced to seek shelter that night,
who had removed their property only to be burned in the
streets or pilfered by gangs of miscreants, whose dis-
honesty no feelings of honesty could restrain when such
an opportunity for plunder occurred. More than 2,000
families, mostly in comfortable circumstances, for this
was the wealthiest and busiest part of the city, were
deprived of their homes, very few having even a change
of linen.

There were but two cases of loss of life: Samuel
Kingston, Esq., who was last seen going into his resi-
dence near Scotch Hill to remove a piano. Confused by

the smoke he wandered into the cellar and met his fate.
The remains of Mrs. Malone were also discovered in the
same vicinity.

The city insurance companies of that day, the
Penn, Firemens, Mutual, Naval and Fire paid losses a-
mounting to $79,800.00 The total insurance, home and
foreign, reached only $870,000.00. The losses of some
individuals ranged from $5,000.00 to $200,000.00 The
list of business firms burned out included 37 commission,
forwarding and wholesale grocery houses; 6 druggists and
chemists; 5 dry-goods dealers; 4 hardware merchants; 2
queensware; 2 bookstores; 2 paper warehouses; 5 boot
and shoe stores; 3 livery stables, and 2 fire-works, in
addition to a large number of minor establishments.

PITTSBURGH IN 1850

Mr. Craig who had been a long time
resident of Pittsburgh, for over
fifty years, wrote a description
of the city, which illustrates the
growth and development of Pittsburgh.

Source: John N. Boucher, ed. in chief. A Century and a
Half of Pittsburgh and Her People. Pittsburgh, 1908,
vol. I, pp. 294-295.

We would be pleased if we could give our readers
an adequate conception of the appearance of the plain
on which our city stands at the time of the first assessment, or even many years later. Those who see Pittsburg in its present not very pleasant aspect, can scarcely imagine its former ragged and broken appearance. We
shall attempt to describe it. The ramparts of Fort
Pitt were still standing and a portion of the officer's
quarters; a substantial brick building was used as a
malt house; the gates were gone, and brick wall called
the revetment which supported two of the ramparts facing
toward the town, and against which the officers used to
play ball, were gone, so that the earth all around had
assumed a natural slope. Outside of the fort on the
side next to the Allegheny river was a large, deep pond,
the favorite resort of wild ducks. Along the south side
of Liberty Street, and extending from the foot of Diamond
Alley to the foot of Fourth Street, was another pond,
from which a deep ditch led the water unto a brick arch
way, leading from Front Street, just below Redoubt Alley,
into the Monongahela. By whom this archway was built I
have never learned. It was no trifling work. The wri-
ter, when a boy, has often played through it. The sides,
which were from three to four feet high, and the top,
were of hard burned bricks, the bottom of flag stones.
Before it was made there must have been a deep gulley
extending up from the river below Redoubt Alley and I
have supposed that when General Grant built the archway
or culvert constructed to facilitate communication between the redoubt and Fort Pitt.
South of Market Street, between Front and Water
Street, was another pond and still another in the square
in front of the St. Charles' Hotel. Finally there was
Hogg's Pond, extending along the north side of Grant's
Hill from Fourth Street up to Seventh. From this last
there was a low, ugly drain, extending down nearly parallel with Wood Street to the river. A stone bridge was
built across this gulley in Front Street probably soon

after the borough was incorporated, because without it
the gulley would be very difficult to pass. We have
now (1850) a beautiful landing along the Monongahela
from the bridge to the point. Fifty years, nay, even
thirty years ago, nothing could be less pleasing to the
eye than the rugged, irregular bank. From the bridge
down to near Wood Street the distance from the lots to
the break of the bank was fifty or sixty feet. At Market Street there was a deep gulley worn into the bank
so that a wagon could hardly pass along. At the mouth
of Chancery Lane there was another chasm in the bank so
that a horse could not pass between the post at the corner of the lot and the precipitous bank. At the mouth
of Ferry Street there was another similar contraction of
the way, so that it required very careful driving for a
wagon to pass along. . . .

THE RAILROAD STRIKE AND RIOT
July, 1877

The railroad strike, which had begun in Baltimore, eventually
spread to Pittsburgh, where the
situation became so chaotic that a
committee of Public Safety was
formed. The establishment of this
committee is described along with
the attempts to establish order.

Source: Sarah H. Killikelly. The History of Pittsburgh,
Its Rise and Progress. Pittsburgh, 1906, pp. 234-236.

On Monday morning, at eleven o'clock, a meeting of
citizens was called to convene at the Chamber of Commerce
to form a Committee of Public Safety to take charge of
the situation, as the city authorities, the Sheriff and
the military seemed powerless. At this meeting the fol-
lowing Committee of Public Safety was appointed: William
G. Johnston, chairman; John Morehead, Paul Hacke, Ralph
Bagaley, George Wilson, J. J. Gillespie, G. Schleiter,
J. G. Weldon, George H. Thurston, James J. Donnell, James
B. Haines, George A. Kelly, F. H. Eaton, J. E. Schwartz,
Joseph Horne, William T. Dunn, R. G. Jones, Dr. McIntosh,
Frank Bisel, John R. McCune, John M. Davis, John B. Jackson, R. C. Grey, Alexander Bradley, Captain Samuel Harper.
On motion, George H. Thurston, George A. Kelly, John
M. Davis were appointed a committee to prepare an address
to the public, and in a short time presented the following, which was adopted and ordered to be at once published.
"The Committee of Public Safety, appointed at the
meeting of citizens held at the Chamber of Commerce, July
twenty-third, deeming that the allaying of excitement is
the first step towards restoring order, would urge upon all
citizens disposed to aid therein the necessity of pur-
suing their usual avocation, and keeping all their employees at work, and would, therefore, request that full
compliance be accorded to this demand of the committee.
The committee are impressed with the belief that the police force now being organized will be able to arrest and
disperse all riotous assemblages, and that much of the
danger of destruction to property has passed, and that an
entire restoration of order will be established. The
committee believe that the mass of industrious workmen of
the city are on the side of law and order, and a number
of the so-called strikers are already in the ranks of the
defenders of the city, and it is quite probable that any
further demonstration will proceed from thieves and simi-

lar classes of population, with whom our working classes
have no affiliation and will not be found among them.
    It is to this end that the committee request that
all classes of business should be prosecuted as usual,
and our citizens refrain from congregating in the streets
in crowds, so that the police of the city may not be
confused in their efforts to arrest rioters, and the military be not restrained from prompt action, if necessary, from fear of injuring the innocent."
    At this meeting Major T. Brent Swearingen was direc-
ted to take charge of organizing the citizens who might
desire to form organizations for the protection of the
city. A Vigilance Committee was also authorized to be
formed under charge of General Negley and Major Swear-
ingen, and establish headquarters at Lafayette Hall.
    In other sections of the country the railroad trou-
bles were increasing and the committee thought best to
call Major General Joe Brown and Colonel Guthrie of the
Eighteenth National Guards, into consultation. Under
their advice a camp was formed of the military at East
Liberty, to be held in readiness for any further outbreak. Mayor McCarthy enrolled five hundred extra police
and issued a proclamation in which he said "I have determined that peace, order and quiet <u>shall be restored</u> to
the community, and to this end call upon all good citizens to come forward at once to the old City Hall and
unite with the police and military now organizing. I
call upon all to continue quietly at their several places of business and refrain from participating in exci-
ted assemblages."
    A proclamation had also been previously issued by
Governor Hartranft, and he had come to Pittsburgh to address the rioters, and subsequently some two or three
thousand troops were ordered by him to Pittsburgh, and
were encamped near East Liberty for several days. Under
these vigorous measures quiet was in a few days restored,
and the railroad riots of Pittsburgh were a thing of the
past, although the Committee of Public Safety continued
to hold sessions and to take steps not only to prevent
any further demonstrations, but to arrest and bring to
punishment a number of prominent rioters. The mistake
of allowing a collection of thieves and similar vagabonds
to assimilate themselves with a mere handful of strikers
and thus become the mob it did was the first error in
the efforts to control the mob. The next was calling out
the military before the civil authorities had exhausted
their power, and the greatest of all was the bringing of
the troops from the east.
    Every step taken until the Committee of Public Safe-
ty took charge of affairs only tended to enrage the working classes, instead of quieting them to a point of reason. It gave demagogues and bad men the opportunity to
play upon the passions of the masses, . . .

PITTSBURGH, THE INDUSTRIAL CITY -- 1884

The following selection describes
Pittsburgh during its hey-day as
the industrial city, par excel-
lence, in the United States.

Source: Willard Glazier. Peculiarities of American
Cities. Philadelphia, 1884, pp. 332-334.

By all means make your first approach to Pittsburgh
in the night time, and you will behold a spectacle which
has not a parallel on this continent. Darkness gives
the city and its surroundings a picturesqueness which
they wholly lack by daylight. It lies low down in a
hollow of encompassing hills, gleaming with a thousand
points of light, which are reflected from the rivers,
whose waters glimmer, it may be, in the faint moonlight,
and catch and reflect the shadows as well. Around the
city;s edge, and on the sides of the hills which encircle
it like a gloomy amphitheatre, their outlines rising
dark against the sky, through numberless apertures, fiery
light stream forth, looking angrily and fiercely up toward the heavens, while over all these settles a heavy
pall of smoke. It is as though one had reached the
outer edge of the infernal regions, and saw before him
the great furnace of Pandemonium with all the lids lif-
ted. The scene is so strange and weird that it will live
in the memory forever. One pictures, as he beholds it,
the tortured spirits writhing in agony, their sinewy
limbs convulsed, and the very air oppressive with pain
and rage.
But the scene is illusive. This is the domain of
Vulcan, not of Pluto. Here, in this gigantic workshop,
in the midst of the materials of his labor, the god of
fire, having left his ancient home on Olympus, and established himself in this newer world, stretches himself be-
side his forge, and sleeps the peaceful sleep which is
the reward of honest industry. Right at his doorway are
mountains of coal to keep a perpetual fire upon his al-
tar; within the reach of his outstretched grasp are fi-
vers of coal oil; and a little further away great stores
of iron for him to forge and weld, and shape into a
thousand forms; and at his feet is the shining river, an
impetuous Mercury, ever ready to do his bidding. Grecian
mythology never conceived of an abode so fitting for the
son of Zeus as that which he has selected for himself on
this western hemisphere. And his ancient tasks were
child's play compared with the mighty ones he has under-
taken to-day.
Failing a night approach, the traveler should

reach the Iron City on a dismal day in autumn, when the
air is heavy with moisture, and the very atmosphere looks
dark. All romance has disappeared. In this nineteenth
century the gods of mythology find no place in daylight.
There is only a very busy city shrouded in gloom. ...
        Pittsburgh is not a beautiful city. That stands to
reason, with the heavy pall of smoke which constantly
overhangs her. But she lacks beauty in other respects.
She is substantially and compactly built, and contains
some handsome edifices; but she lacks the architectural
magnificence of some of her sister cities; while her
suburbs present all that is unsightly and forbidding in
appearance, the original beauties of nature having been
ruthlessly sacrificed to utility.
        Pittsburgh is situated in western Pennsylvania,
in a narrow valley at the confluence of the Allegheny
and Monongahela rivers, and at the head of the Ohio,
and is surrounded by hills rising to the height of four
or five hundred feet. These hills once possessed rounded
outlines, with sufficient exceptional abruptness to lend
them variety and picturesqueness. But they have been le-
veled down, cut into, sliced off, and ruthlessly marred
and mutilated, until not a trace of their original outlines remain. Great black coal cars crawl up and down
their sides, and plunge into unexpected and mysterious
openings, their sudden disappearance lending, even in
daylight, an air of mystery and diablerie to the region.
Railroad tracks gridiron the ground everywhere, debris
of all sorts lies in heaps, and is scattered over the
earth, and huts and hovels are perched here and there,
in every available spot. There is no verdure--nothing
but mud and coal, the one yellow the other black. And
on the edge of the city are the unpicturesque outlines
of factories and foundries, their tall chimneys belching
forth columns of inky blackness, which roll and whirl in
fantastic shapes, and finally lose themselves in the
general murkiness above.
        The tranquil Monongahela comes up from the south,
alive with barges and tug boats; while the swifter current of the Allegheny bears from the oil regions, at the
north, slight-built barges with their freights of crude
petroleum. Oil is not infrequently poured upon the
troubled waters, when one of these barges sinks, and
its freight, liberated from the open tanks, refuses to
sink with it, and spreads itself out on the surface of
the stream.
        The oil fever was sorely felt in Pittsburgh, and
it was a form of malaria against which the smoke-laden
atmosphere was no protection. During the early years of
the great oil speculatoon the city was in a perpetual
state of excitement. Men talked oil upon the streets,
in the cars and counting-houses, and no doubt thought
of oil in church. Wells and barrels of petroleum, and

shares of oil stock were the things most often mentioned.
. . .
        The city boasts of universities, colleges, hospi-
tals and asylums, and the Convent of the Sisters of Mercy is the oldest house of the order in America. .There
are also two theatres, an Opera House, an Academy of
Music, and several public halls.
        But it is not any of these which has made the city
what she is, or to which she will point with her greatest
pride. The crowning glory of Pittsburgh is her monster
iron and glass works. One-half the glass produced in
all the United States comes from Pittsburgh. This important business was first established here in 1787, by
Albert Gallatin, and it has increased since then to giant
proportions. Probably, not less than one hundred millions of bottles and vials are annually produced here,
besides large quantities of window glass. The best wine
bottles in America are made here, though they are inferior to those of French manufacture. A great number
of flintglass works turn out the best flint glass produced in the country.
        In addition to these glass works--which, though
they employ thousands of workmen, represent but a frac-
tion of the city's industries--there are rolling mills,
foundries, potteries, oil refineries, and factories of
machinery. All these works are rendered possible by the
coal which abounds in measureless quantities in the immediate neighborhood of the city. All the hills which
rise from the river bank of Pittsburgh have a thick stra-
tum of bituminous coal running through them, which can
be mined without shafts, or any of the usual accessories
of mining. All that is to be done is to shovel the coal
out of the hill-side, convey it to cars or by means of
an inclined plane to the factory or foundry door, and
dump it, ready for use. In fact, these hills are but
immense coal cellars, ready filled for the convenience
of the Pittsburgh manufacturers. True, in shoveling the
coal out of the hill-side, the excavations finally become
galleries, running one, two or three miles directly into
the earth. But there is neither ascent nor descent; no
lowering of miners or mules in great buckets down a deep
and narrow shaft, no elevating of coal through the same
means. It is all like a great cellar, divided into
rooms, the ceilings supported by arches of the coal itself. Each miner works a separate room, and when the
room is finished, and that part of the mine exhausted
the arches are knocked away, pillars of large upright
logs substituted, the coal removed, and the hill left
to settle gradually down, until the logs are crushed
and flattened. . . .
        Pittsburgh is a city of workers. From the proprie-
tors of these extensive works, down to the youngest ap-
prentices, all are busy; and perhaps the higher up the

scale. the harder the work and the greater the worry.
A man who carries upon his shoulders the responsibility
of an establishment whose business amounts to millions
of dollars in a year; who must oversee all departments
of labor, accurately adjust the buying of the crude materials and the scale of wages on the one hand, with the
price of the manufactured article on the other, so that
the profit shall be on the right side; and who at the
same time shall keep himself posted as to all which bears
any relation to his business, has no time for leisure or
social pleasures, and must even stint his hours of necessary rest.

Pittsburgh illustrates more clearly than any other
city in America the outcome of democratic institutions.
There are no classes here except the industrious classes;
and no ranks in society save those which have been created by industry. The mammoth establishments, some of
them perhaps in the hands of the grandsons of their found-
ers, have grown from small beginnings, fostered in their
growth by industry and thrift. The great proprietor of
to-day, it may have been, was the "boss" of yesterday,
and the journeyman of a few years ago, having ascended
the ladder from the lowest round of apprenticeship.
Industry and sobriety are the main aids to success.

The wages paid are good, for the most part, vary-
ing according to the quality of the employment, some of
them being exceedingly liberal. The character of the
workmen is gradually improving, though it has not yet
reached the standard which it should attain. Many are
intelligent, devoting their spare time to self-improve-
ment, and especially to a comprehension of the relations
of capital and labor, which so intimately concern them,
and which they, more than any other class of citizens,
except employers, need to understand, in order that
they may not only maintain their own rights, but may
avoid encroaching on the rights of others. . . .

NEW CITY CHARTER, 1901

Pursuant to the Act of March 7th,
1901, the City enacted a new Charter, replacing the Mayor as chief
executive officer with a City Recorder. The selections from the
Charter printed below indicate the
other Executive Departments and
the manner of conducting municipal business. This form of municipal government was retained for
only two years.

Source: Charter Ordinance, City of Pittsburgh to Carry
into Effect the Act of March 7th, 1901. Pittsburgh,
1901, pp. 1-7, 32-35.

AN ORDINANCE--To carry into effect in the City of Pittsburgh an Act of Assembly entitled, "An Act for the government of cities of the second class," approved the
7th day of March, 1901; referring to the qualifications
and appointments of the City Recorder; establishing the
Departments of Public Safety, Public Works, Collector of
Delinquent Taxes, Assessors, City Treasurer, City Controller, Law, Charities and Correction, and Sinking Fund
Commission; creating and fixing Bureaus and the titles
thereof, and subordinate officers and offices; prescribing the mode of their election or appointment, defining
the duties and powers of such, fixing the amount of bonds
to be given, and allotting the various Bureaus and other
officers to the proper Departments.

SECTION 1. Be it ordained and enacted by the City
of Pittsburgh, in Select and Common Councils assembled,
and it is hereby ordained and enacted by the authority
of the same. That on and after the passage of this Ordinance the executive power of the City of Pittsburgh
shall be vested in a City Recorder and the Departments
authorized by an Act of Assembly entitled, "An Act for
the government of cities of the second class," approved
the 7th day of March, A. D. 1901.

CITY RECORDER.

SECTION 2. The City Recorder shall possess such
qualifications, perform such duties and make such appointments as are now or hereafter may be prescribed by
law; he shall give bond to the City of Pittsburgh in the
sum of twenty-five thousand dollars; he shall be and is
hereby authorized and empowered to appoint and employ one
suitable person to act as chief clerk for the City Re-

corder and in the City Recorder's office, one suitable
person to act as assistant clerk for the City Recorder
and in the City Recorder's office, one person to act as
filing clerk for the City Recorder and in the City Recorder's office, one person to act as stenographer for
the City Recorder, and one person to act as messenger for
said City Recorder; all of said persons to perform such
service and do such work as the said City Recorder may
direct; all such appointees shall receive such salary or
compensation as is now or may hereafter be fixed by ordinance.

 SECTION 3. The following Departments are hereby
established, in accordance with said Act:
 First: DEPARTMENT OF PUBLIC SAFETY.
 Second: DEPARTMENT OF PUBLIC WORKS.
 Third: DEPARTMENT OF COLLECTOR OF DELINQUENT TAXES.
 Fourth: DEPARTMENT OF ASSESSORS.
 Fifth: DEPARTMENT OF CITY TREASURER.
 Sixth: DEPARTMENT OF CITY CONTROLLER.
 Seventh: DEPARTMENT OF LAW.
 Eighth: DEPARTMENT OF CHARITIES AND CORRECTION.
 Ninth: SINKING FUND COMMISSION.

DEPARTMENT OF PUBLIC SAFETY.

 SECTION 4. The Department of Public Safety shall
be under the charge, direction, control and administration of one person, who shall be the head thereof, and
whose official title shall be Director of the Department
of Public Safety: he shall be appointed by, and be subject and responsible to, the City Recorder; he shall give
bond to the City of Pittsburgh in the sum of fifty thousand dollars; and possess such qualifications, perform
such duties, and manage, administer, supervise and control such matters as are now or hereafter may be prescribed by law. The said director shall be and is hereby authorized to appoint and employ such persons, at
such compensation, as is now or may hereafter be fixed
by ordinance.

 SECTION 5. The following Bureaus shall be attached
to, be part of, and be under the control, direction and
supervision of the Department of Public Safety.

BUREAU OF POLICE.

 SECTION 6. There shall be and is hereby created a
bureau to be known as the Bureau of Police, which bureau
shall have the care, management, administration and supervision of all the police force or forces, officer or
officers (including park police and ordinance officers),
the preservation of the peace, and all matters pertaining to police affairs, and shall be attached to and
be under the control, direction and supervision of the
Department of Public Safety, and shall consist of such
persons, at such compensation, as is now or may hereafter

be fixed by ordinance. This bureau shall at all times
be subject to such rules and regulations as may be prescribed by the City Recorder and the Director of the
Department of Public Safety.

/There follows the other Bureaus under the Director
of Public Safety, including Bureau of Detectives, Bureau
of Fire, Bureau of Health, Bureau of Electricity, Bureau
of Building Inspection, and Bureau of Plumbing, Gas
Fitting and House Drainage. Then follows the duties
of all other Directors of Departments./

GENERAL PROVISIONS

SECTION 39. Each head or director of the aforesaid departments of the City of Pittsburgh shall be at
least thirty (30) years of age, and have been a citizen
and inhabitant of the State of Pennsylvania for five (5)
years next before his appointment or election as director, and each director shall reside in the City of Pittsburgh during the term for which he shall have been elected or appointed, and he shall take and subscribe to the
oath prescribed by Article VII of the Constitution of
this State, which oath shall be administered by and
filed with the City Recorder. . . .

The bonds required to be given by such heads or directors of said departments, shall be approved in the
model required by law, to-wit; by the City Recorder and
the City Controller, and shall be deposited with and kept
in the custody of the City Recorder, and said bonds may
be examined and revised annually by the City Recorder,
and, if required, new bonds shall be given.

SECTION 40. The several departments provided for
in this Ordinance shall be entitled to such other clerks
and employees as the City Recorder and the heads or directors thereof may deem necessary.

SECTION 41. The offices for each department shall
be provided by the city, and shall be open each secular
day, excepting legal holidays, from 9 a. m. until 5 p. m.
for the transaction of public business. . . .

SECTION 42. The City Recorder may sign all warrants and all other official papers and documents (except ordinances and resolutions of Councils), with a
stamp to be adopted by him, and which shall be a _fac_ _si-_
mile of his signature, and said warrants and all other
official papers and documents when signed with said stamp
and attested hereinafter set forth, shall be accepted by
the City Controller and the City Treasurer and all other
persons, and acted upon the same as if signed by the
said City Recorder with ink in his own proper handwriting as heretofore. Provided, that he, the said City
Recorder shall personally affix his said signature by and
with said stamp to any and all of said warrants and official papers and documents he signs by and with said
stamp as aforesaid; and provided further, that said sig-

nature shall not be valid or accepted as aforesaid, unless the same be attested in ink by the written signature of the City Recorder's Chief Clerk or Assistant Clerk in his own proper handwriting.

SECTION 43. Suitable and proper books of account shall be kept by all of said departments, wherein shall appear a full and clear statement of the condition of public business, showing an account of all money received or expended, and generally all matters or things in which the public may be interested. The City Controller shall have and is hereby given authority to prescribe from time to time the mode in which all public accounts shall be kept.

SECTION 44. The City Recorder and the directors of the several departments shall each have and are hereby given the right and authority to demand a bond from the head of each of the various bureaus and their subordinates, in such sum as such City Recorder or such director shall determine, conditioned for the faithful performance of the duties and obligations imposed from time to time upon such heads of bureaus and subordinates.

SECTION 45. All heads of bureaus, employees and clerks of said city, shall be citizens of the United States, and shall be residents in and inhabitants of the City of Pittsburgh, and shall reside therein during their term of service and employment, and shall have resided in said city at least six months prior to such appointment. Provided, however, that if the City Recorder and several directors of departments shall find it impossible to obtain sufficient or satisfactory laborers, experts or bureau officials, then and in that case they shall have the right to employ laborers, experts or bureau officials residing outside the City of Pittsburgh; and provided further, that employees of the Department of Charities and Correction, doing service at the City Home and Hospitals at Marshalsea need not be residents of the City of Pittsburgh during the time of their said employment.
. . .

PITTSBURGH CHARTER ORDINANCE OF 1902

In accordance with "An Act for the
government of cities of the Second
Class," the Pittsburgh Council
passed an ordinance establishing
its government under a mayor, executive departments, and a city
council. It went into effect in
1903.

Source: Digest of the General Ordinances and Laws of
the City of Pittsburgh to March 1, 1938. Athens, Pa.,
1938, pp. 56-59.

PITTSBURGH CHARTER ORDINANCE OF 1902

SECTION 162. An ordinance.--To carry into effect
in the City of Pittsburgh an Act of Assembly entitled,
"An Act for the government of cities of the second
class," approved the 7th day of March, 1901; referring
to the qualifications and appointments of the /City Re-
corder/Mayor; establishing the Departments of Public
Safety, Public Works, Collector of Delinquent Taxes,
Assessors, City Treasurer, City Controller, Law, Charities and Correction, and Sinking Fund Commission; creating and fixing Bureaus and the titles thereof, and subordinate officers and offices; prescribing the mode of
their election or appointment, defining the duties and
powers of such; fixing the amount of bonds to be given,
and allotting the various Bureaus and other officers to
the proper departments.--Charter Ordinance of 1902,
No. 450, Title.

SECTION 163. Executive Power vested in Mayor and
departments.--Be it ordained and enacted by the City of
Pittsburgh, in Select and Common Councils assembled, and
it is hereby ordained and enacted by the authority of the
same; That on and after the passage of this ordinance the
executive power of the City of Pittsburgh shall be vested
in a Mayor and the departments authorized by an Act of
Assembly entitled "An Act for the government of cities
of the second class," approved the 7th day of March,
A. D., 1901.--Sec. 1, Charter Ordinance of 1902, No. 450,
ap. Jan. 7, 1902, O. B. 14, page 307.

Section 164. The Mayor.--The Mayor shall possess
such qualifications, perform such duties and make such
appointments as are now or hereafter may be prescribed
by law; he shall give bond to the City of Pittsburgh in
the sum of twenty-five thousand dollars; he shall be and
is hereby authorized and empowered to appoint and employ
one suitable person to act as chief clerk for the Mayor

and in the Mayor's office, one suitable person to act as
assistant clerk for the Mayor, and in the Mayor's office, one person to act as filing clerk for the Mayor
and in the Mayor's office, one person to act as stenographer for the Mayor, and one person to act as messenger
for said Mayor; all of said persons to perform such service and do such work as the said Mayor may direct; all
such appointees shall receive such salary or compensation
as is now or may hereafter be fixed by ordinance.--Sec.
2, Charter Ordinance of 1902, No. 450.

SECTION 165. Executive Departments.--The following
departments are hereby established in accordance with
said Act.

First: Department of Public Safety.
Second: Department of Public Works.
Third: Department of Collector of Delinquent Taxes.
Fourth: Department of Assessors.
Fifth: Department of City Treasurer.
Sixth: Department of City Controller
Seventh: Department of Law.
Eighth: Department of Public Welfare.
Ninth: Sinking Fund Commission.
Tenth: Department of Public Health.
Eleventh: Department of Supplies.
Twelfth: Art Commission.
Thirteenth: Department of City Planning.
Fourteenth: Department of City Development.
Fifteenth: Department of Transit.
Sixteenth: Department of Lands and Buildings.--Sec.
3, Charter Ordinance of 1902, No. 450, amended by Or-
dinance of 1909, No. 6. . . .

SECTION 209. Committees of Council.--That it shall
be and is hereby made the duty of the Presidents of the
Select and Common Councils upon the enactment of this
ordinance, and at or before the first regular meeting of
Councils after the organization thereof in each and
every second year hereafter, to appoint from the members
of said Councils the following joint standing committees,
viz:

SECTION 210. Committees as of 1937:
Committee on Finance
Committee on Public Works
Committee on Public Service and Surveys
Committee on Filtration and Water
Committee on Parks and Libraries
Committee on Public Safety
Committee on Public Welfare
Committee on Health and Sanitation
Committee on Hearings

SECTION 211. Jurisdiction of committees, as set
forth in Charter Ordinance of 1901.--The Presidents of
Select and Common Councils shall be members of all joint

standing committees, and, in addition thereto, all said
committees shall consist of twelve members of the Common Council and nine members of the Select Council, except the Committee on Finance, which, in addition to the
Presidents of Councils, shall have nine members of the
Common Council and six members of the Select Council; the
Committee on Surveys, which, in addition to the Presidents of Councils, shall have fifteen members of the
Common Council and twelve members of the Select Council;
and the Committee on Libraries, which, in addition to
the Presidents of the Council and two members of the
Select Council.

The Committee on Finance shall have charge of and
jurisdiction over all ordinances, resolutions, bills, papers and all matters relating to the finances, taxation
and indebtedness of the city, and the appropriation of
moneys, or the payment of moneys not provided for by previous authority of law; the exoneration, release or satisfaction of any claims held by the city; the creation
of offices or positions of any kind; the regulation of
salaries, fixing the number and pay of employes; the care
and control of the public funds and all other legal and
financial business of the city government, and such other
business as may be referred to it by either branch of the
City Councils; provided, however, that where money has
been specifically appropriated by the City Councils for
any of the purposes of the departments of the city government; that thereafter any matter relating thereto
shall be referred to the committee of the proper department, and the said committee shall then have complete
charge and jurisdiction thereof.

The Committee on Public Works shall have charge of
and jurisdiction over all ordinances, resolutions, bills
or papers pertaining to the Department of Public Works,
which either branch of Councils may direct. The Committee on Public Works shall be divided into three (3)
sub-committees as follows: Water, Highways and Sewers,
and Property.

The Committee on Public Safety shall have charge
of and jurisdiction over all matters of every kind and
character pertaining to the business of the Department
of Public Safety, including all matters relating to police affairs, to fire, to city telegraphs, the inspection of buildings, fire escapes, and all such other matters pertaining to the Department of Public Safety as
either branch of the City Councils may direct.

The Committees on Charities and Correction shall
have charge of and jurisdiction over all ordinances, resolutions, bills or papers affecting or pertaining to the
Department of Charities and Correction.

The Committee on Filtration shall have charge of
and jurisdiction over all ordinances, resolutions, plans
and specifications relating to the erection and construc-

tion of the filtration plant for the City of Pittsburgh.

The Committee on Corporations shall have charge of and jurisdiction over all ordinances, resolutions, bills and papers relating to the grant of franchises, rights and privileges to corporations, firms or individuals, and the exercise of same by such corporations, firms or individuals.

The Committee on Surveys shall have charge of and jurisdiction over all ordinances, resolutions and bills pertaining to the laying out, establishing the grade and vacating of public highways of the city.

The Committee on Health and Sanitation shall have charge of and jurisdiction over all ordinances, resolutions, bills and papers relating to the public health, the inspection of gas fitting, plumbing and house drainage, and the maintenance and improvement of hygenic conditions in the city.

The Committee on Parks shall have charge of and jurisdiction over all ordinances, resolutions and bills pertaining to the public parks.

The Committee on Bridges shall have charge of and jurisdiction over all ordinances, resolutions and bills pertaining to the public bridges.

The Committee on Libraries shall have charge of and jurisdiction over all ordinances, resolutions and bills pertaining to the public libraries. The members thereof shall be members of the Board of Trustees of the Carnegie Library, in accordance with the terms of the deed of trust of Andrew Carnegie.

The Committee on Hearings arranges for and has charge of all general public hearings before the Council.

The chairman of the above named committees shall be ex-officio members of all the sub-committees appointed by them.

A majority of the members of the Committees on Finance, Public Works, Public Safety, Charities and Correction, Filtration, Corporations, Health and Sanitation, Parks, Bridges and Libraries, and one-third of the members of the Committee on Surveys, shall constitute a quorum for the transaction of business by the several committees respectively. . . .

MAYOR MCNAIR'S RESIGNATION
October 6, 1936

Democratic Mayor William McNair,
who had been constantly feuding
with his own party members,
failed to gain approval of his new
appointee as City Treasurer. The
Mayor finally resigned on October
6, 1936. Mr. McNair's spectacular
actions, as well as the background
of the dispute, are indicated in
the two articles that follow.

Source: New York Times, February 17, 1935, Section IV,
6:7 and October 7, 1936, 9:3.

PITTSBURGH, Feb. 14--Bills to "rip" Mayor William
N. McNair from office were introduced this week in the
House of the Legislature and at the same time, under
different auspices, another measure was presented in the
State Senate for a city manager charter for Pittsburgh,
modeled after the Cincinnati plan.

Sentiment has been shown lately for removal of the
Mayor, the first Democrat elected to the office here in
a quarter of a century. His own party organization is
behind the purely ripper bill. It is commonly accepted
that the patronage feature is largely present in this,
the Mayor not only having refused to play ball with the
leaders to any considerable extent, but also having
fought them in a number of instances. Having been elected principally by Republican votes, he gave some of his
principal cabinet posts to members of that party.

But the Mayor has proved a disappointment to many
of his supporters of both parties. It is not that he
has done anything scandalously wrong--his honesty is
generally conceded. His judgment, however, has been obviously bad in a number of instances, as in the dismissal
of competent employes and replacement of them with individuals having no qualifications for the work. In a little more than a year he has had four safety directors.

One of the loudest cries against the Mayor came
when he caused a number of sanitary inspectors to be furloughed, numerous complaints arising that the health of
the city was imperiled. There were many calls for his
impeachment at that time.

There was a factor against impeachment, however,
from the Democratic standpoint. Automatically the Republican President of Council, Robert Garland, would become Mayor until the election of such an officer, and
this still complicates the situation for the Democrats.

The Senate of the Legislature is still in the hands of
Republicans, and it is felt that if a member of that
party is enabled to reach the Mayoralty by a ripper, the
Republican Senate would be slow to join in any action
that would shorten his stay.

* * *

PITTSBURGH, Oct. 6--William N. McNair ended his
tumultuous Mayorality career today with an unceremonious
one sentence resignation and went back to the law office
from which he emerged four years ago.

The Mayor stepped aside, he explained, to end the
financial chaos arising out of the City Council's refusal
to confirm his appointee for City Treasurer. Without a
treasurer the city's payrolls were frozen and thousands
were going unpaid.

Only a few hours after Mr. McNair submitted his
resignation to City Clerk Edward B. Schofield members of
the Council held a special meeting and designated Cornelius D. Scully, their president, to succeed him.

Mr. Scully, who managed Mr. McNair's successful
Mayoralty campaign in 1932, took the oath of office immediately. His first act was to reappoint James P. Kirk,
the City Treasurer whose dismissal led to the financial
turmoil after the Council refused to confirm the successor named by Mr. McNair, William B. Foster.

Although elected on the Democratic ticket, Mr. Mc-
Nair broke with the party shortly after taking office,
and he has been in almost constant warfare with the Democratic Council over appointments and policies. Mr. Kirk
is the Democratic County Chairman.

Mr. McNair spoke cheerfully of his resignation,
which merely stated:

"I hereby resign from the office as Mayor of the
city of Pittsburgh, to be effective immediately."

He ended his reign as Chief Executive, during which
he nearly always was in the limelight through a series
of escapades which both awed and cheered his constit-
uents.

Sitting in his law office, the former Mayor said
"he simply had to give up and let the Council run the
city -- that's the only way it can be run."

Asked why he resigned, Mr. McNair gave this reply:

"Because the city has to function. The employees
at Mayview Hospital are not paid, the payrolls in the
parks are not paid; there will be a big police payroll
today; we're running out of soda ash at the filtration
plant to counteract the mine acid in the water supply.

"I was fighting the many interests, tramping on
too many people's toes."

After his inauguration, Mr. McNair put his desk in
the lobby, "so the people can reach me." He climbed a

ladder to determine the draught and, while perched there, made a speech on the "single tax," his political hobby. A few days later he removed his desk to the executive offices because of the draught.

He appeared for one week on the local stage as a fiddle player, once rode a steer through a downtown street and again called in an orchestra and hummed to the strains of the music while signing bonds.

Several months ago he went to jail for two hours for refusing to refund a $100 fine which a man claimed had been improperly collected.

More recently he went to jail again on a misbehavior charge, but a grand jury refused to indict him.

The Mayor's term would have expired Jan. 1, 1938. Mr. Scully will serve until that time, with a new Mayor being elected in November.

POSTWAR URBAN DEVELOPMENT
December, 1947

Pittsburgh was quick to realize
what years of neglect due to the
Depression period in the 1930's,
followed by the Second World War,
had done in regard to further de-
terioration of the central core.
As a result, representatives of
the private sector of the economy
quickly began to work toward a reconstruction and rehabilitation
of the inner city. The description of the goals of the project
indicate the growing awareness of
urban problems by prominent industrial, business and labor
leaders.

Source: New York _Times_, December 19, 1947, Section VIII,
1:1.

PITTSBURGH, Dec. 18--This is the first major city
to rebuild and to try to make itself depression-proof,
fifteen leading executives in civic, industrial, research, mining, banking and retailing revealed here today at a luncheon meeting at the Duquesne Club. They
provided the first consolidated report on the joint management, labor, government, financial and merchants
many-sided community redevelopment program which is being pushed to completion without fear of setbacks due to
economic recession.

Describing the fifteen-point program, Dr. Edward
R. Weidlein, director of Mellon Institute and chairman
of the Allegheny Conference on Community Development,
said, "These things are absolutely a necessity and
could not be deferred. Everything we've got scheduled
is moving along rapidly. Back of this program are builders and 'doers' who are not deterred by possible changes
in the business cycle."

Advantages stressed

Dr. Weidlein stressed the practical advantages of
the work and said that ample facts now are available to
prove that increased productivity in Pittsburgh plants
will be one of the important benefits from industrial
health improvement aspects. But other luncheon guests
pointed out that old established companies here are ex-
panding and diversifying their products, new companies

are coming in to further diversify industrial output
here and save shipping costs under increased freight
rates, which would apply if there plants were located
elsewhere.

In addition large increases in total Pittsburgh
employment are envisaged as these expansions make use of
a large reservoir of potential women employes discovered
during a four-county inventory of social and economic
resources. . . .

Step by step, the Pittsburgh plan is correcting
now all of the things that can possibly be corrected
to bulwark maximum future employment, assure steady annual incomes, avoid future setbacks due to preventable
business losses, stabilize year-round production, improve engineering and merchandising practices, increase
foreign trade, speed traffic and transportation and improve the "livability" of the town, they said.

New York experts in medical, scientific, economic
and engineering fields have finished their preliminary
surveys of conditions which can be corrected, they continued. Dr. Weldlein declared, "In going ahead now on
their recommendations, we are putting first things first,
admitting we must recognize that progress must be made
through practical methods, rather than through discussion
of vague theories. These steps comprise a vast "broaden-
ing of the base of Pittsburgh's future prosperity."

In this billion-dollar program industrial expendi-
tures far outshadow disbursements of taxpayers' funds
through civic and governmental agencies in a ratio of
about two to one, a tabulation of projects disclosed.
Among spectacular industrial projects, the $120,000,000
construction plan of pooled resources of Pittsburgh Consolidated Coal Company and Standard Oil Company of New
Jersey is now under way with a pilot plant being built
to show how to standardize processes of making gasoline,
fuel oil and alcohol from coal. Jones & Laughlin Steel
Corporation is spending $4,500,000 for "smoke-free" new
boiler plants replacing forty-three old boilers which
created smoke hazards in the past. In all, two-thirds
of the J & L $107,000,000 modernization plan is being
spent here. Non-commercial aircraft have already started
to use the new $20,000,000 greater Pittsburgh airport
located on a 1,500-acre site double the size of New
York's La Guardia Field. Allis-Chalmers Manufacturing
Company is now completing a $2,000,000 plant expansion
program here. Weirton Steel Company is spending all of
$100,000,000 within sixty miles of Pittsburgh and Nation-
al Supply Company is spending $20,000,000, all in Pitts-
burgh.

PITTSBURGH DOWNTOWN IMPROVEMENT
June, 1953

Pittsburgh had been one of the
first of the major American cities to recognize, and begin to
act on the deteriorating problems of the inner city. Public
and private building plans contributed to a $1,000,000,000
campaign. As a result many new
buildings and roadways were being constructed. The improvement in property values was im-
pressive.

Source: New York _Times_, June 8, 1953, 44:1.

PITTSBURGH, June 7--Building managers and owners
at long last are coming into full realization of their
great stake in the preservation and improvement of
"downtown" or central business districts in the fact of
a decentralization movement which has gained ground during the post war period in nearly every metropolitan
area.

The challenge offered by suburban satellite expan-
sion has stirred them, for the sake of their own holdings
and as a matter of civic interest. to participate active-
ly in urban redevelopment programs.

The progress and aims of these plans to give new
life to the established business centers will be the
chief topics of the forty-sixth annual convention of
the National Association of Building Owners and Managers,
which opened here today.

The delegates are making a first-hand study of
Pittsburgh's rebirth under a $1,000,000,000 improvement
scheme involving office skyscrapers, expressways, parks,
shopping centers and adequate parking facilities.

Civic Progress Is Hailed

The changes have been taking shape rapidly in the
past two or three years, and this city is deemed to have
made more progress in downtown redevelopment and planning
than almost any other.

The transformation has centered in the new Mellon
Square and in the Old Golden Triangle districts.

The valuable land has been acquired by the city
with the assistance of a $4,000,000 gift for that purpose,
made by the Mellon interests. On one side of it already
has been built the forty-story U. S. Steel-Mellon sky-

scraper, and on the opposite side finishing touches now
are being placed on the thirty-story Alcoa Building of
the Aluminum Company of America.

Both structures rise skyward without setbacks in
an intensive use of sites such as would not be permitted
in New York or other cities with structure-building-
bulk regulations. Naturally the United States Steel
edifice makes extensive use of steel on the interior and
exterior, and the Alcoa tower is sheathed with aluminum.

Mellon Square, in addition to its park and large
fountains, will have four floors of underground parking
space. Close by are the new Carlton Hotel and the Bige-
low Apartments with adjoining parking garage.

The Golden Triangle is undergoing an even more im-
pressive metamorphosis.

Pittsburgh's re-development work will be described
to the convention delegates by W. P. Snyder, president
of the Alleghany Regional Advisory Board.

Decentralization problems in general, and ways of
combating this movement, will be outlined by several
speakers, including William H. Doughty, head of the Chicago Association of Building Managers. . . .

PITTSBURGH RIOT, April 5-8, 1968

In the wake of Dr. Martin Luther
King's assassination riots broke
out in black sections of cities
throughout the nation. Pittsburgh's disorders were so severe
that National Guardsmen had to be
called in. The extent of the dis-
order, and the force necessary to
reestablish order can be seen in
the following description.

Source: New York _Times_, April 8, 1968, 1:6.

PITTSBURGH, April 7--National Guardsmen, state and
city police restored relative calm to the city's Negro
Hill district tonight following three days of widespread
looting and fire bombing by Negro gangs.
"It's calm and quiet," police said at 10 P.M., although there were scattered reports of looting and fire
bombing in several other sections of the city.
Twenty-two hundred National Guardsmen and 300
state police moved into this tense steel capital this
afternoon to bolster the city's beleagured 1,400-man police force.
A total of 3,112 Guardsmen were expected here by
early morning, while 1,500 more were on standby alert in
armories throughout western Pennsylvania.
A reporter toured the Hill district on foot at 10
P.M. and reported the streets nearly deserted except for
lawmen and occasional stragglers who were unaware of a
dawn-to-dusk curfew imposed by Gov. Raymond P. Shafer.
"I am gratified that the violence seems to be
lessening and am please with the cooperation between go-
vernments at the state, local and Federal levels," Governor Shafer said.
He said he had been in touch with the Justice Department, which "in turn has informed President Johnson
of the situation here in Pennsylvania."
Calm descended on the Hill district a short time
after a third contingent of guardsmen arrived in the area
to reinforce troopers sent in earlier.
Nearly every store along a five-block stretch of
Centre Avenue was looted, burned or had its windows
smashed. Debris littered the street and the smell of
burnt wood permeated the night air.
At least 24 persons, including two guardsmen, three
firemen, four policemen and a reporter, were injured
seriously enough to require hospital treatment.
A police spokesman said 568 adults and juveniles

had been arrested since the disturbances began Friday.
He said there were 164 fires--95 of them today--and arson was suspected in all of them.

Governor Shafer ordered in the Guard and state police after declaring a state of emergency that outlawed
street gatherings of more than 10 persons, prohibited
service stations from selling gasoline that is not
"pumped directly into tanks of vehicles" and established
a 7 P.M. to 5 A.M. curfew. Liquor sales in the city had
been banned previously.

The Hill district is a 20-square-block area bor-
dering on Pittsburgh's downtown Golden Triangle of new
office buildings and high apartments. Its 40,000 residents are 90 per cent Negro and have an unemployment rate
four times as high as the rest of the city.

Guardsmen with fixed bayonets marched 30 abreast
through the Hill to clear the streets this afternoon.
They were stoned and pelted with bottles from rooftops
sporadically, as were police and firemen.

At one point smoke from one of the many fires was
so thick that police called for gas masks.

"We can't get within a block of it /the fire/ the
smoke is so dense," a policeman said.

A reporter in the Hill district said the main tar-
get of the looters appeared to be liquor stores, groceries and establishment handling clothing. Much of the
looting and fire bombing centered on three main thorough-
fares--Centre, Bedford and Wylie Avenues.

A memorial march for the slain Rev. Dr. Martin Luther King, Jr. was delayed for 35 minutes waiting for
police reinforcements. About 1,000 marchers, guarded
by helmeted police with three-foot billy clubs moved
10 abreast down the hill toward the downtown area. They
held hands and sang "We Shall Overcome."

For the third straight day bands of Negroes, mostly
youths, broke store fronts, looted, hurled fire-bombs and
stopped traffic.

In several confrontations stones were hurled at
the police as they rushed in to control the gangs. Police vans were kept busy hauling violators to station
houses.

Some looters used shopping carts taken from grocery stores they had broken into to haul away their loot.
Others loaded automobiles with merchandise.

"There must be more than 1,000 persons running wild
on the Hill," a police spokesman said. "It's getting
harder and harder to cope with."

For a brief time, Mayor Barr ordered bridges link-
ing the downtown section and the North Side closed to
traffic.

Thousands of white church-goers, out in their Sunday finery, stared at the guardsmen as the church bells
rang out in the area, signalling the start of memorial
services for Dr. King.

BIBLIOGRAPHY

The works cited in the Bibliography have been carefully selected
to indicate the major sources to
be consulted for further research
on the growth and development of
Pittsburgh. Materials listed in
the Primary Sources section are
those which have been published
since the early development of
the city. The Secondary Sources
have been published during the
nineteenth and twentieth centuries.
The variety of works was chosen to
provide a cross-section of the information on the social, economic
and political life of the city.
Students should also consult the
Reader's Guide to Periodical Literature and Social Science and
Humanities Index for further articles on Pittsburgh.

PRIMARY SOURCES

By-Laws and Ordinance of the City of Pittsburgh, and the
    Acts of the Assembly Relating Thereto; With Notes
    and References to Judicial Decisions Thereon and
    an Appendix, Relating to Several Subjects Connec-
    ted with the Laws and Police of the City Corpora-
    tion. Pittsburgh, 1928.

Carnegie Library of Pittsburgh. Pennsylvania. A Reading
    List for the Use of Schools, with Special Reference
    to Indian Warfare and the Local History of Pitts-
    burgh. Pittsburgh, 1911.

Charter Ordinance. City of Pittsburgh. To Carry Into
    Effect the Act of March 7th, 1901. Pittsburgh,
    1901.

Dedication Souvenir Comprising a History and Description
    of the Public Library, Music Hall, Art Gallery and
    Scientific Halls Founded by Andrew Carnegie. Pitts-
    burgh, 1885.

A Digest of the Acts of Assembly and a Code of the Ordi-
    nances of the City of Pittsburgh. Pittsburgh, 1869.

A Digest of the Acts of Assembly Relating to, and the

General Ordinances of the City of Pittsburgh from 1804
    to January 1, 1897. . . . . Pittsburgh, 1897.

A Digest of the Acts of Assembly Relating to and the
    General Ordinances of the City of Pittsburgh from
    1804 to November 12, 1908 (and the Ordinances of
    Allegheny). Pittsburgh, 1908.

A Digest of the Acts of Assembly, the Codified Ordinan-
    ces, . . . Adopted October 6, 1859; and a Digest
    of Other Ordinances Now in Force. Pittsburgh,
    1860.

A Digest of the Acts of Assembly Relating to, and the
    General Ordinances of the City of Pittsburgh, From
    1804 to September 1, 1886. . . Harrisburg, Pa.,
    1887.

Digest of the General Ordinances and Laws of the City of
    Pittsburgh to March 1, 1938. Athens, Pa., 1938.

A Digest of the Ordinances of the City of Pittsburgh and
    of the Acts of Assembly Relating Thereto. Pitts-
    burgh, 1845.

A Digest of Ordinances of the City of Pittsburgh to Which
    is Prefixed a Collection of the Acts of Assembly
    Relating to the Corporation. Pittsburgh, 1849.

The First Seven Years, A Report of the Housing Authority
    of the City of Pittsburgh for the Years 1937-1944.
    Pittsburgh, 1945.

Guthrie, George Wilkins. The Pending Subway Ordinance.
    Address...Before the Pittsburgh Chamber of Com-
    merce, December 14, 1911. Pittsburgh, 1911.

Holdsworth, John Thom. Report of the Economic Survey of
    Pittsburgh. Pittsburgh, 1912.

Jones, Samuel. Pittsburgh in the Year Eighteen Hundred
    and Twenty-Six, Containing Sketches, a Topographi-
    cal, Historical and Statistical; Together with a
    Directory of the City. Pittsburgh, 1826.

Olmsted, Frederick Law. Pittsburgh, Main Thoroughfares
    and the Down Town District; Improvements Necessary
    to Meet the City's Present and Future Needs.
    Pittsburgh, 1911.

Ordinances Creating a Pension Board and Pension Fund for
    the Pensioning of Employees of the City of Pitts-
    burgh. . . . Pittsburgh, 1915.

Ordinances of the Select and Common Councils of . . .
    Pittsburgh, . . . With the Acts of Assembly Re-
    lating to the City, . . . /Note: These volumes
    were issued each year in the 19th and 20th cen-
    turies./

Pittsburgh and Western Pennsylvania: Their Industries
    and Commerce, Resources and Prospects. Pittsburgh,
    1885.

Pittsburgh Area Transportation Study. Final Report.
    Study Conducted Under the Sponsorship of the Com-
    monwealth of Pennsylvania. Department of Highways,
    County of Allegheny /and/ City of Pittsburgh in
    Cooperation with United States Department of Com-
    merce, Bureau of Public Roads. Pittsburgh, 1961-
    1963. 2 vols.

Pittsburgh Business Review; A Review of Business and
    Economic Conditions in the Pittsburgh District.
    vol. 1- date. December, 1930 - date. Pittsburgh,
    1930 - date.

Pittsburgh, Pa. Carnegie Library. Annual Report. vol.
    1 - date. 1896 - date.

Pittsburgh Chamber of Commerce. Annual Report. 1881 -
    date. Pittsburgh, 1882 - date.

------------------------------. Pittsburgh and the Sea-
    way, A Preliminary Report. Pittsburgh, 1956.

Pittsburgh. City Planning Commission. Basic Data on
    Income and Expenditures for Public Works Improve-
    ments, 1930-1945, as Related to a Six-Year Program
    of Public Works Maintenance, 1946 to 1951; . . .
    Pittsburgh, 1945.

Pittsburgh. Civic Commission. City Planning for Pitts-
    burgh; Outline and Procedure. Pittsburgh, 1910.

Pittsburgh City Planning Commission. Pittsburgh; Ground-
    work and Inventory for the Master Plan. Pitts-
    burgh, 1945.

------------------------------------. Report. . . 1911/12
    - date. Pittsburgh, 1912 - date.

------------------------------------. What Will Pitts-
    burgh Make of Itself? Pittsburgh, 1945.

Pittsburgh Civil Service Commission. Annual Report.
    1907/08 - date. Pittsburgh, 1908 - date.

Pittsburgh Common Council. <u>Municipal Record</u>. <u>Minutes</u>
<u>of the Proceedings</u>. vols. 1 - 44. 1868 - 1911.
Superseded June, 1911 by the <u>Municipal Record of</u>
<u>the Council</u>.

———————————————————————. <u>Municipal Record</u>. <u>Minutes</u>
<u>of Proceedings</u>. vol. 45 - date. 1911 - present.

Pittsburgh. Controller. <u>Annual Report of the City Con-</u>
<u>troller</u>. 1874/75 - date. Pittsburgh, 1875 -
date. 1878/79 not published.

<u>Pittsburgh First</u>. vol. 1 - date. May 24, 1919 - date.
Pittsburgh, 1919 - date. Official organ of the
Pittsburgh Chamber of Commerce.

Pittsburgh Health Bureau. <u>Annual Report</u>. 1873/74 -
1907. Pittsburgh, 1874 - 1909. 1900 - 1906,
1908 - 1909 not published. Continued as Pittsburgh. Public Health Department. <u>Annual Report.</u>

Pittsburgh. Parks Bureau. <u>Annual Report</u>. 1936 - present. Pittsburgh, 1937 - .

Pittsburgh. Public Education Board. <u>Annual Report</u>.
Pittsburgh, 1913 - present.

—————————————————————————————————. <u>Annual Report of</u>
<u>the Superintendent, Pittsburgh Public Schools</u>,
1869/70 - date. Pittsburgh, 1870 - date.

Pittsburgh. Public Health Department. <u>Annual Report</u>.
1910/11 - date. Pittsburgh, 1911 - present.

Pittsburgh Recreation Bureau. <u>Report</u>. 1935 - date.
1937 - date. Title: <u>Annual Report</u>.

Pittsburgh. Select Council. <u>Municipal Record</u>. <u>Minutes</u>
<u>of the Proceedings</u>. vol. 1 - 44, 1868 - 1911.
Pittsburgh, 1868 - 1911. Superseded by: Pittsburgh. Council. <u>Municipal Record</u>. 1868 - 1880/81
have title: <u>Municipal Record; Minutes of Proceed-</u>
<u>ings of the Select and Common Councils</u>.

Pittsburgh. Sesqui-Centennial Committee. <u>Official Mu-</u>
<u>nicipal Program of the Sesqui-Centennial Celebra-</u>
<u>tion of the City of Pittsburgh. September Twenty-</u>
<u>seventh to October third and November twenty-fifth</u>,
<u>Nineteen Hundred and Eight</u>. Pittsburgh, 1908.

<u>Public Health Laws of the City of Pittsburgh; An Anno-</u>
<u>tated Compilation of the Laws, Regulations and Or-</u>
<u>dinances of the State of Pennsylvania and the City</u>

of Pittsburgh Governing the Administration of Public Health in Pittsburgh. Pittsburgh, 1910.

SECONDARY SOURCES

American Historical Company, Inc. History of Pittsburgh
and Environs. New York, 1922. This series of
essays presents important aspects of the history
of the area.

Bakewell, Mary Ella. Of Long Ago; The Children and the
City. Pittsburgh, 1937. This is a good analysis
of some citizens of Pittsburgh and their contributions to its growth.

Baldwin, Leland Dewitt. Pittsburgh: The Story of a City.
Pittsburgh, 1937. A study of the early history
of the city is presented.

Boucher, John Newton, editor in chief. A Century and a
Half of Pittsburgh and Her People. Pittsburgh,
1908. 4 vols. This is a series of articles concerning various institutions, organizations and
groups in Pittsburgh as well as biographical
sketches of leading figures in the city's history.

Brisonnette, Wesley Smith. Pittsburgh, Songs of the Mo-
ther's Sons. Boston, 1926.

Callahan, James M. The Pittsburgh-Wheeling Rivalry for
Commercial Headship on the Ohio. Columbus, Ohio,
1913.

Catholic Historical Society of Western Pennsylvania.
Catholic Pittsburgh's One Hundred Years, . . .
Chicago, 1943.

Church, Samuel Harden. A Short History of Pittsburgh,
1758-1908. New York, 1908.

Cowan, John Pryor, compiler. Great Men; Their Esteem
for a Great City. . . Pittsburgh, 1919.

Craig, Neville B. The History of Pittsburgh, with a
Brief Notice of Its Facilities of Communication,
and other Advantages for Commercial and Manufacturing Purposes. Pittsburgh, 1851.

Dahlinger, Charles William. Fort Pitt. Pittsburgh,
1922. A detailed study of the Fort and early settlement is presented.

------------------------. <u>Pittsburgh; A Sketch of Its
Early Social Life</u>. New York, 1916.

Daughters of the American Revolution. Pennsylvania,
     Allegheny County. Fort Pitt Society. <u>Fort Du-
     quesne and Fort Pitt. Early Names of Pittsburgh
     Streets</u>. Pittsburgh, 1953.

Glover, Eli Sheldon, ed. <u>History of Western Pennsylvania
     Previous to the Civil War</u>. Chicago, 1910. This
     is a good study of the entire western part of the
     state emphasizing Pittsburgh.

Fleming, George Thornton. <u>History of Pittsburgh and En-
     virons</u>. New York, 1922. 3 vols. This is a de-
     tailed study of the historical development of the
     city along with sketches of many of its leading
     citizens during the era involved.

Frey, Laura C. <u>The Land in the Fork: Pittsburgh, 1753-
     1914</u>. Philadelphia, 1955. The author discusses
     the highlights of Pittsburgh's development.

Gazette Times, Pittsburgh. <u>The Story of Pittsburgh.
     Pittsburgh and Vicinity, Illustrated</u>. Pittsburgh,
     1908.

Gregg, O. Ormsby. <u>Pittsburgh, Her Advantageous Position
     and Great Resources as a Manufacturing and Commer-
     cial City</u>. Pittsburgh, 1845.

Groat, Dick and Bill Surface. <u>The World Champion Pitts-
     burgh Pirates</u>. New York, 1961. These sports-
     writers discuss the development of the team and the
     story of their winning the National League pennant
     and the World Series in 1960.

Hall, J. Morton. <u>America's Industrial Centre. Pitts-
     burgh's Great Industries and Its Enormous Develop-
     ment in the Leading Products of the World</u>. Pitts-
     burgh, 1891.

Harper, Frank C. <u>Pittsburgh: Forge of the Universe, A
     Review of Pittsburgh's Matchless Two Hundred Year
     History; The Rise of Economic Democracy and Indus-
     trial Liberalism and the Great Civic Upsurge in
     Capitalism's Key City</u>. New York, 1957. This
     study presents a history of the city from the po-
     litical, social and economic viewpoint.

----------------. <u>Pittsburgh of Today, Its Resources and
     People</u>. New York, 1931. 4 vols. The author pre-
     sents the political history along with details of

the industrial and economic growth of the City
and many of the men who made it.

James, Alfred Procter. Dreams in the Forest: Decision
at the Forks and C. M. Stotz. Defense in the
Wilderness. Pittsburgh, 1958. This is an interesting study of the early development of Pittsburgh during the colonial and early national period.

Johnston, William Graham. Life and Reminiscences from
Birth to Manhood of William G. Johnston. Pittsburgh and New York, 1901.

Killikelly, Sarah H. The History of Pittsburgh, Its
Rise and Progress. Pittsburgh, 1906. This study
is valuable because of the citation of many sources some of which had not been utilized previously.

Kussart, Mrs. Sarepta. The Early History of the Fifteenth Ward of the City of Pittsburgh. Bellevue,
Pennsylvania, 1925.

Lieb, Frederick George. The Pittsburgh Pirates. New
York, 1948. This is a study of the growth and
development of the team.

Lanpher, Erwin Eurgen. City of Pittsburgh, Pennsylvania,
Its Water Works. . . Pittsburgh, 1930.

Lorant, Stephan, ed. Pittsburgh; The Story of an American City. Garden City, New York, 1964. This is
a series of separate essays dealing with the historical development and current aspects of the
city.

Macartney, Clarence Edward Noble. Right Here in Pittsburgh. Pittsburgh, 1937.

Marsh, Daniel L. The Challenge of Pittsburgh. New York,
1917. This is a study of the city and its needs.

Mathews, Philip. History of the Pittsburgh Bureau of
Governmental Research. Pittsburgh, 1936.

Miller, Annie Clark. Chronicles of Families, Houses and
Estates of Pittsburgh and Its Environs. Pittsburgh, 1927.

Nevin, Adelaide Mellier. The Social Mirror; A Character
Sketch of the Women of Pittsburgh and Vicinity
During the First Century of the Country's Exis-
tence. Pittsburgh, 1888.

Pittsburgh in 1816. Compiled by the Carnegie Library
        of Pittsburgh on the one hundredth anniversary of
        the granting of the City Charter. Pittsburgh,
        1916.

Powell, Lyman Pierson, ed. Historic Towns of the Middle
        States. New York, 1901.

Shames, Sally Oleon. David L. Lawrence, Mayor of Pitts-
        burgh: Development of a Political Leader. Pitts-
        burgh, 1938.

Slippy, John Clifford. Civic Pittsburgh. Pittsburgh,
        1927. An analysis of the development of the city
        and its civic aspects.

Smith, Percy Frazer. Memory's Milestones: Reminiscences
        of Seventy Years of a Busy Life in Pittsburgh.
        Pittsburgh, 1918.

-------------------. Notable Men of Pittsburgh and Vi-
        cinity. Pittsburgh, 1901.

The Story of the Sesquicentennial Celebration of Pitts-
        burgh, July 4, September to October 3 and November
        25, 1908. . . Pittsburgh, 1910.

Swetnam, George. Pittsylvania Country. New York, 1951.

Thurston, George Henry. Pittsburgh and Allegheny in the
        Centennial Year. Pittsburgh, 1876.

United States. Works Progress Administration. Pennsyl-
        vania. . . . Tales of Pioneer Pittsburgh: Spon-
        sored by Western Pennsylvania Committee on Folk-
        lore, Philadelphia, 1937.

Vermorcken, Elizabeth M. Pittsburgh Portraits. Pitts-
        burgh, 1955.

Wilson, Erasmus, ed. Standard History of Pittsburgh,
        Pennsylvania. Chicago, 1898. This is a series
        of essays by various contributors.

                        JOURNAL ARTICLES

Andrews J. Cutler. "The Pittsburgh Gazette -- A Pioneer
        Newspaper." Western Pennsylvania Historical Maga-
        zine. XV (1932), 293-307.

Benswanger, William F. "Professional Baseball in Pitts-
        burgh," Western Pennsylvania Historical Magazine.

XXX, nos. 1-2 (1947), 9-14.

Betts, Lillian W. "Pittsburgh: A City of Brain and
    Brawn." Outlook, LXIX, 17-33.

Bothwell, Margaret Pearson. "Killbuck and Killbuck
    Island." Western Pennsylvania Historical Magazine.
    XLIV (December, 1961), 343-360.

Brackenridge, Hugh Henry. "Brackenridge's Account of
    Pittsburgh in 1786,"/Extract from Pittsburgh Ga-
    zette, July 29, 1786./ Monthly Bulletin. Carnegie
    Library of Pittsburgh. VII (1902), 257-261; 288-
    290, 332-335.

"The Centennial Commemoration of Pittsburgh's Big Fire
    of April 10, 1845," Western Pennsylvania Historical
    Magazine. XXVIII (1945), 1-81.

Crall, F. Frank. "A Half Century of Rivalry Between
    Pittsburgh and Wheeling." Western Pennsylvania
    Historical Magazine. XIII (1930), 237-255.

Ewing, Robert M. "Washington's Western Journeys and
    Their Relation to Pittsburgh." Western Pennsyl-
    vania Historical Magazine. V (1922), 220-235.

Fearon, Henry Bradsham. "Another View of Pittsburgh in
    1817. /Extract from Fearon's 'Sketches of Ameri-
    ca'/ Monthly Bulletin. Carnegie Library of Pitts-
    burgh. VII (1902), 155-166.

Ilisevich, Robert D. "Louis Kossuth's Visit to Pitts-
    burgh in 1852." Western Pennsylvania Historical
    Magazine. XL, no. 2 (Summer, 1957), 77-87.

James, James Alton. "Pittsburgh, a Key to the West
    During the American Revolution." Ohio Archaeologi-
    cal and Historical Quarterly. XXII (1913), 64-79.

Liggett, Walter W. "Pittsburgh - Metropolis of Corrup-
    tion." Plain Talk. VII (1930), 129-152.

McKeever, Edward M. "Earlier Lawrenceville." Western
    Pennsylvania Historical Magazine. V (1922), 277-
    286.

Oliver, John W. "Pittsburgh's Awakening One Hundred
    Years Ago." Western Pennsylvania Historical Ma-
    gazine. XIII (1930), 189-194.

"Pittsburgh and Vicinity in 1761." Western Pennsylvania
    Historical Magazine. III (1920), 198-200.

Potter, John. "The Place of Pittsburgh in History."
    Western Pennsylvania Historical Magazine. IX
    (1926), 1-23.

Scaife, William Lucien. "A Glimpse of Pittsburgh."
    Atlantic Monthly. LXXXVII, 83-88.

Sheedy, Morgan M. "Ten Days on Historic Ground. Early
    and Late Days at the Pittsburgh Point." Western
    Pennsylvania Historical Magazine. V (1922), 135-

Simpson, Mrs. "Reminiscences of Early Pittsburgh."
    Western Pennsylvania Historical Magazine. IV
    (1921), 243-245.

Tefft, B. F. "Pittsburgh in 1848." Western Pennsylvania
    Historical Magazine. XVII (1934), 190-197.